THE COMPLETE POEMS OF CAVAFY

RAE DALVEN ALSO TRANSLATED AND EDITED

Poems by Joseph Eliyia AND *Modern Greek Poetry.*

THE COMPLETE POEMS OF CAVAFY

TRANSLATED BY RAE DALVEN · WITH AN INTRODUCTION BY W. H. AUDEN

HARCOURT, BRACE & WORLD, INC. NEW YORK

A Harvest Book

 Library of Congress Catalog Card Number: 60-10936. Printed in the United States of America.

E F G H I

TO MY MOTHER

ACKNOWLEDGMENTS

I owe a special debt to Professor Procope S. Costas, of Brooklyn College, who went over the entire manuscript with a scholar's thoroughness and made valuable suggestions. To Sophia Papadaky, of Athens, I owe a debt of another kind. It was she who sent me the copy of Cavafy's *Poems,* which I used for my translations, and the texts of eighteen of the early poems which were available only in magazines.

Others to whom I owe a debt of gratitude for their help and encouragement are Dr. Mary Karahali, W. H. Auden, Andre Michalopoulos, Dr. Clarence R. Decker, Charles Angoff, Professor Constantinos Trypanis, of Oxford, Mark Van Doren, Stephanos Zotos, Dr. Basil Valaoras, Dr. Basil Vlavianos, Alfred Kreymborg, David Kalugin, the Right Reverend Bishop of Ancona Sideris, and Dr. Nicholas Parlamis.

I would like to thank Hogarth Press, London, for releasing their exclusive rights to translating into English the poems of Cavafy.

For biographical material, I have drawn freely on *The Life and Work of Cavafy* by Michael Peridis and *Cavafy and His Epoch* by Stratis Tsirkas. I have also used the two volumes on Cavafy by Timos Malanos. I have consulted three earlier translations of Cavafy's poems: the translation in English by John Mavrogordato of the poems in the Greek edition and the translations in French of the same poems by Georges Papoutsakis and by Marguerite Yourcenar and Constantin Dimaras. The full titles of these volumes are listed in the Bibliography.

INTRODUCTION BY W. H. AUDEN

Ever since I was first introduced to his poetry by the late Professor R. M. Dawkins over thirty years ago, C. P. Cavafy has remained an influence on my own writing; that is to say, I can think of poems which, if Cavafy were unknown to me, I should have written quite differently or perhaps not written at all. Yet I do not know a word of Modern Greek, so that my only access to Cavafy's poetry has been through English and French translations.

This perplexes and a little disturbs me. Like everybody else, I think, who writes poetry, I have always believed the essential difference between prose and poetry to be that prose can be translated into another tongue but poetry cannot.

But if it is possible to be poetically influenced by work which one can read only in translation, this belief must be qualified.

There must be some elements in poetry which are separable from their original verbal expression and some which are inseparable. It is obvious, for example, that any association of ideas created by homophones is restricted to the language in which these homophones occur. Only in German does *Welt* rhyme with *Geld,* and only in English is Hilaire Belloc's pun possible.

> When I am dead, I hope it may be said:
> 'His sins were scarlet, but his books were read.'

When, as in pure lyric, a poet "sings" rather than "speaks," he is rarely, if ever, translatable. The "meaning" of a song by Campion is inseparable from the sound and the rhythmical values of the actual words he employs. It is conceivable that a genuine bilingual poet might write what, to him, was the same lyric in two languages, but if someone else were then to make a literal translation of each version into the language of the other, no reader would be able to recognize their connection.

On the other hand, the technical conventions and devices of verse can be grasped in abstraction from the verse itself. I do not have to know Welsh to become excited about the possibility of applying to English verse the internal rhymes and alliterations in which Welsh verse is so rich. I may very well find that they cannot be copied exactly in English, yet discover by modifying them new and interesting effects.

Another element in poetry which often survives translation is the imagery of similes and metaphors, for these are derived, not from local verbal habits, but from sensory experiences common to all men.

I do not have to read Pindar in Greek in order to appreciate the beauty and aptness with which he praises the island of Delos.

> . . . motionless miracle of the
> wide earth, which mortals call Delos, but the

> blessed on Olympus, the far-shining star of
> dark-blue earth.

When difficulties in translating images do arise, this is usually because the verbal resources of the new language cannot make the meaning clear without using so many words that the force of the original is lost. Thus Shakespeare's line

> The hearts that spanielled me at heels

cannot be translated into French without turning the metaphor into a less effective simile.

None of the translatable elements in poetry which I have mentioned so far applies, however, to Cavafy. With the free relaxed iambic verse he generally uses, we are already familiar. The most original aspect of his style, the mixture, both in his vocabulary and his syntax, of demotic and purist Greek, is untranslatable. In English there is nothing comparable to the rivalry between demotic and purist, a rivalry that has excited high passions, both literary and political. We have only Standard English on the one side and regional dialects on the other, and it is impossible for a translator to reproduce this stylistic effect or for an English poet to profit from it.

Nor can one speak of Cavafy's imagery, for simile and metaphor are devices he never uses; whether he is speaking of a scene, an event, or an emotion, every line of his is plain factual description without any ornamentation whatsoever.

What, then, is it in Cavafy's poems that survives translation and excites? Something I can only call, most inadequately, a tone of voice, a personal speech. I have read translations of Cavafy made by many different hands, but every one of them was immediately recognizable as a poem by Cavafy; nobody else could possibly have written it. Reading any poem of his, I feel: "This reveals a person with a unique perspective on the world." That the speech of self-disclosure should be translatable seems to me very odd, but I am convinced that it is. The conclusion I draw is that the only quality which all human beings without exception possess is uniqueness: any characteristic, on the other hand, which one individual can be recognized as having in common with another, like red hair or the English language, implies the existence of other individual qualities which this classification excludes. To the degree, therefore, that a poem is the product of a certain culture, it is difficult to translate it into the terms of another culture, but to the degree that it is the expression of a unique human being, it is as easy, or as difficult, for a person from an alien culture to appreciate as for one of the cultural group to which the poet happens to belong.

But if the importance of Cavafy's poetry is his unique tone of voice, there is nothing for a critic to say, for criticism can only make comparisons. A unique tone of voice cannot be described; it can only be imitated, that is to say, either parodied or quoted.

To be writing an introduction to Cavafy's poetry, therefore, is to be in the embarrassing position of knowing that what one writes can only be of interest to people who have not yet read him; once they have, they will forget it as completely as, when one makes a new friend at a party, one forgets the person who made the introduction.

Cavafy has three principal concerns: love, art, and politics in the original Greek sense.

Cavafy was a homosexual, and his erotic poems make no attempt to conceal the fact. Poems made by human beings are no more exempt from moral judgment than acts done by human beings, but the moral criterion is not the same. One duty of a poem, among others, is to bear witness to the truth. A moral witness is one who gives true testimony to the best of his ability in order that the court (or the reader) shall be in a better position to judge the case justly; an immoral witness is one who tells half-truths or downright lies: but it is not a witness's business to pass verdict. (In the arts, one must distinguish, of course, between the lie and the tall story that the audience is not expected to believe. The tall-story teller gives himself away, either by a wink or by an exaggerated poker face: the born liar always looks absolutely natural.)

As a witness, Cavafy is exceptionally honest. He neither bowdlerizes nor glamorizes nor giggles. The erotic world he depicts is one of casual pickups and short-lived affairs. Love, there, is rarely more than physical passion, and when tenderer emotions do exist, they are almost always one-sided. At the same time, he refuses to pretend that his memories of moments of sensual pleasure are unhappy or spoiled by feelings of guilt. One can feel guilty about one's relation to other persons—one has treated them badly or made them unhappy—but nobody, whatever his moral convictions, can honestly regret a moment of physical pleasure as such. The only criticism that might be made is one that applies to all poets, namely, that Cavafy does not, perhaps, fully appreciate his exceptional good fortune in being someone who can transmute into valuable poetry experiences which, for those who lack this power, may be trivial or even harmful. The sources of poetry lie, as Yeats said, "in the foul rag-and-boneshop of the heart," and Cavafy illustrates this by an anecdote:

> The fulfillment of their deviate, sensual delight
> is done. They rose from the mattress,
> and they dress hurriedly without speaking.
> They leave the house separately, furtively; and as
> they walk somewhat uneasily on the street, it seems
> as if they suspect that something about them betrays
> into what kind of bed they fell a little while back.

> But how the life of the artist has gained.
> Tomorrow, the next day, years later, the vigorous verses
> will be composed that had their beginning here.
> ("*Their Beginning*")

But what, one cannot help wondering, will be the future of the artist's companion?

Cavafy's attitude toward the poetic vocation is an aristocratic one. His poets do not think of themselves as persons of great public importance and entitled to universal homage, but, rather, as citizens of a small republic in which one is judged by one's peers and the standard of judgment is strict. The young poet Eumenes is depressed because, after struggling for two years, he has only managed to write one idyll. Theocritus comforts him thus:

> And if you are on the first step,
> you ought to be proud and pleased.
> Coming as far as this is not little;
> what you have achieved is great glory. . . .
> To set your foot upon this step
> you must rightfully be a citizen
> of the city of ideas.
> And in that city it is hard
> and rare to be naturalized.
> In her market place you find Lawmakers
> whom no adventurer can dupe. . . .
> ("*The First Step*")

His poets write because they enjoy writing and in order to give aesthetic satisfaction, but they never exaggerate the importance of aesthetic satisfaction.

> Let the flippant call me flippant.
> In serious matters I have always been
> most diligent. And I will insist that
> no one is more familiar than I
> with Fathers or Scriptures, or the Synodical Canons.
> In each of his doubts,
> in each difficulty concerning church matters,
> Botaneiatis consulted me, me first of all.
> But exiled here (may the malevolent Irene Doukaina
> suffer for it), and dreadfully bored,
> it is not at all peculiar that I amuse myself
> composing sestets and octets—
> that I amuse myself with mythological tales
> of Hermes, Apollo, and Dionysus,
> or the heroes of Thessaly and the Peloponnese;
> and that I compose impeccable iambics.

such as—permit me to say—Constantinople's men of
letters cannot compose.
This very accuracy, probably, is the cause of their censure.
("A *Byzantine Noble in Exile Writing Verses*")

Cavafy is intrigued by the comic possibilities created by the indirect relation of poets to the world. While the man of action requires the presence of others here and now, for without a public he cannot act, the poet fabricates his poem in solitude. He desires, it is true, a public for his poem, but he himself need not be personally related to it and, indeed, the public he most hopes for is composed of future generations which will only come into being after he is dead. While he is writing, therefore, he must banish from his mind all thoughts of himself and of others and concentrate on his work. However, he is not a machine for producing verses, but a human being like other human beings, living in a historical society and subject to its cares and vicissitudes. The Cappadocian poet Phernazis is composing an epic on Darius and is trying to imagine the feelings and motives which led Darius to act as he did. Suddenly his servant interrupts him to say that Rome and Cappadocia are at war.

Phernazis is impatient. How unfortunate!
At a time when he was positive that with his "Darius"
he would distinguish himself, and shut forever
the mouths of his critics, the envious ones.
What a delay, what a delay to his plans.

But if it were only a delay, it would still be all right.
But let us see if we have any security at all
in Amisus. It is not a very well-fortified city.
The Romans are the most horrible enemies.
Can we get the best of them, we
Cappadocians? Is that ever possible?
Can we measure ourselves in a time like this against legions?
Mighty Gods, protectors of Asia, help us.—

Yet amid all his agitation and the trouble,
the poetic idea persistently comes and goes.—
The most probable, surely, is arrogance and drunkenness;
Darius must have felt arrogance and drunkenness.
("*Darius*")

Aside from those dealing with his personal experiences, the settings of Cavafy's poems are seldom contemporary. Some are concerned with the history of Ancient Greece, one or two with the fall of Rome, but his favorite historical periods are two: the age of the Greek satellite kingdoms set up by Rome after the Alexandrian Empire had fallen to pieces, and the period of Constantine and his successors when Christianity had just triumphed over paganism and become the official religion.

Of these periods he gives us a number of anecdotes and character vignettes. His Panhellenic world is politically powerless, and in it, therefore, politics are regarded with cynical amusement. Officially, the satellite kingdoms are self-governing, but everyone knows that the rulers are puppets of Rome. Political events that are immensely important to the Romans, like the Battle of Actium, mean nothing to them. Since they must obey in any case, why should they care what name their master bears?

> The news of the outcome of the naval battle, at Actium,
> was most certainly unexpected.
> But there is no need to compose a new address.
> Only the name needs to be changed. There, in the last
> lines, instead of "Having liberated the Romans
> from the ruinous Octavius,
> that parody, as it were, of Caesar,"
> now we will put, "Having liberated the Romans
> from the ruinous Antony."
> The whole text fits in beautifully.
>
> ("*In a Township of Asia Minor*")

There are some, like the Syrian Demetrius Sôtêr, who dream of restoring their country to its former greatness, but they are forced to realize that their dream is vain.

> He suffered, he felt much bitterness in Rome
> as he sensed in the talk of his friends,
> young people of prominent houses,
> amid all the delicacy and politeness
> that they kept showing to him, the son
> of the King Seleucus Philopator—
> as he sensed however that there was always
> a covert indifference to the hellenized dynasties;
> that had declined, that are not for serious works . . .
>
> If only he could find a way to get to the East,
> to succeed in escaping from Italy— . . .
>
> Ah, if only he could find himself in Syria!
> He was so young when he left his country,
> that he can barely remember its face.
> But in his thought he always studied it
> as something sacred you approach with adoration,
> as a vision of a lovely land, as a spectacle
> of Greek cities and harbors.—
>
> And now?
> Now despair and grief.

The young men in Rome were right.
It is not possible for dynasties to survive
that the Macedonian Conquest gave rise to.

No matter: He himself had tried,
he had struggled as much as he could.
And in his dark discouragement,
one thing alone he reckons
with pride, that, even in his failure,
to the world he shows the same indomitable manliness.

The rest—were dreams and vain efforts.
This Syria—scarcely looks like his own country,
it is the land of Heracleides and Balas.

("*Of Demetrius Sôtêr, 162–150 B.C.*")

As this poem illustrates, Cavafy is one of the very few poets who can write a patriotic poem that is not embarrassing. In most poetic expressions of patriotism, it is impossible to distinguish what is one of the greatest human virtues from the worst human vice, collective egoism.

The virtue of patriotism has generally been extolled most loudly and publicly by nations that are in the process of conquering others, by the Romans, for example, in the first century B.C., the French in the 1790's, the English in the nineteenth century, and the Germans in the first half of the twentieth. To such people, love of one's country involves denying the right of others, of the Gauls, the Italians, the Indians, the Poles, to love theirs. Moreover, even when a nation is not actively aggressive, the genuineness of its patriotic feelings remains in doubt so long as it is rich, powerful, and respected. Will the feeling survive if that nation should become poor and of no political account and aware, also, that its decline is final, that there is no hope for the return of its former glory? In this age, no matter to which country we belong, the future is uncertain enough to make this a real question for us all, and Cavafy's poems more topical than, at first reading, they seem.

In Cavafy's Panhellenic world, there is one great object of love and loyalty of which defeat has not deprived them, the Greek language. Even peoples to whom it had not originally been their native tongue have adopted it, and the language has become all the richer for having had to accommodate itself to sensibilities other than Attic.

The inscription, as usual, in Greek;
not exaggerated, not pompous—
lest the proconsul who is always poking about
and reporting to Rome misconstrue it— . . .
Above all I charge you to see to it
(Sithaspes, in God's name, let this not be forgotten)
that after the words King and Savior,

there be engraved in elegant letters, Philhellene.
Now don't try your clever sallies on me,
your "Where are the Greeks?" and "Where is anything Greek
behind Zagros here, beyond Phraata?"
Since so many others more barbarous than we
write it, we too shall write it.
And finally do not forget that at times
sophists from Syria visit us,
and versifiers, and other wiseacres.
So we are not un-Greek, I reckon.
("*Philhellene*")

In his poems about the relations between Christians and Pagans in the age of Constantine, Cavafy takes no sides. Roman paganism was worldly in the sense that the aim of its ritual practices was to secure prosperity and peace for the state and its citizens. Christianity, while not necessarily despising this world, has always insisted that its principal concern was elsewhere: it has never claimed to guarantee worldly prosperity to believers, and it has always condemned excessive preoccupation with success as a sin.

So long as worship of the Emperor as a god was required by law of all citizens, to become a Christian meant to become a criminal. In consequence, the Christians of the first four centuries A.D., though subject like everybody else to the temptations of the Flesh and the Devil, had been spared the temptation of the World. One could become converted and remain a thorough rascal, but one could not be converted and remain a gentleman.

But after Constantine, it was the Christian who had a better chance than the Pagan of getting on in the world, and the Pagan, even if not persecuted, who became the object of social ridicule.

In one of Cavafy's poems the son of a pagan priest has become a Christian convert.

O Jesus Christ, my daily effort
is to observe the precepts
of Thy most holy church in every act of mine,
in every word, in every single thought.
And all those who renounce Thee,
I shun them.—But now I bewail;
I lament, O Christ, for my father
even though he was—a horrible thing to say—
a priest at the accursed Serapeum.
("*Priest at the Serapeum*")

In another, the Emperor Julian comes to Antioch and preaches his self-invented neopagan religion. But to the citizens of Antioch, Christianity has become the conventional religion which they hold without letting it interfere in any way with their amusements, and they merely laugh at him as a puritanical old fuddy-duddy.

> Was it ever possible that they should renounce
> their lovely way of life; the variety of their
> daily amusement; their magnificent theater . . .
>
> To renounce all these, to turn to what after all?
>
> To his airy chatter about false gods;
> to his tiresome self-centered chatter;
> to his childish fear of the theater;
> his graceless prudery; his ridiculous beard?
>
> Ah most surely they preferred the CHI,
> ah most certainly they preferred the KAPPA; a hundred times.
>
> ("*Julian and the People of Antioch*")

I hope these quotations have given some idea of Cavafy's tone of voice and his perspective on life. If a reader find them unsympathetic, I do not know how one can argue against him. Since language is the creation of a social group, not of an individual, the standards by which it can be judged are relatively objective. Thus, when reading a poem in one's native tongue, one can find the sensibility personally antipathetic and yet be compelled to admire its verbal manifestation. But when one is reading a translation, all one gets is the sensibility, and either one likes it or one does not. I happen to like Cavafy's very much indeed.

CONTENTS

THE COMPLETE POEMS OF CAVAFY

DESIRES

Like beautiful bodies of the dead who had not grown old
and they shut them, with tears, in a magnificent mausoleum,
with roses at the head and jasmine at the feet—
that is how desires look that have passed
without fulfillment; without one of them having achieved
a night of sensual delight, or a moonlit morn.

VOICES

Ideal and dearly beloved voices
of those who are dead, or of those
who are lost to us like the dead.

Sometimes they speak to us in our dreams;
sometimes in thought the mind hears them.

And for a moment with their echo other echoes
return from the first poetry of our lives—
like music that extinguishes the far-off night.

SUPPLICATION

The sea took a sailor to its deep.—
His mother, unsuspecting, goes to light

a tall candle before the Virgin Mary
for his speedy return and for fine weather—

and always she cocks her ear to windward.
But while she prays and implores,

the icon listens, solemn and sad, knowing well
that the son she expects will no longer return.

THE FIRST STEP

The young poet Eumenes
complained one day to Theocritus:
"I have been writing for two years now
and I have done only one idyll.
It is my only finished work.
Alas, it is steep, I see it,
the stairway of Poetry is so steep;
and from the first step where now I stand,
poor me, I shall never ascend."
"These words," Theocritus said,
"are unbecoming and blasphemous.
And if you are on the first step,
you ought to be proud and pleased.
Coming as far as this is not little;
what you have achieved is great glory.
For even this first step
is far distant from the common herd.
To set your foot upon this step
you must rightfully be a citizen
of the city of ideas.
And in that city it is hard
and rare to be naturalized.
In her market place you find Lawmakers
whom no adventurer can dupe.
Coming as far as this is not little;
what you have achieved is great glory."

AN OLD MAN

In the inner room of the noisy café
an old man sits bent over a table;
a newspaper before him, no companion beside him.

And in the scorn of his miserable old age,
he meditates how little he enjoyed the years
when he had strength, the art of the word, and good looks.

He knows he has aged much; he is aware of it, he sees it,
and yet the time when he was young seems like
yesterday. How short a time, how short a time.

And he ponders how Wisdom had deceived him;
and how he always trusted her—what folly!—
the liar who would say, "Tomorrow. You have ample time."

He recalls impulses he curbed; and how much
joy he sacrificed. Every lost chance
now mocks his senseless prudence.

. . . But with so much thinking and remembering
the old man reels. And he dozes off
bent over the table of the café.

CANDLES

The days of our future stand before us
like a row of little lighted candles—
golden, warm, and lively little candles.

The days gone by remain behind us,
a mournful line of burnt-out candles;
the nearest ones are still smoking,
cold candles, melted and bent.

I do not want to look at them; their form saddens me,
and it saddens me to recall their first light.
I look ahead at my lighted candles.

I do not want to turn back, lest I see and shudder—
how quickly the somber line lengthens,
how quickly the burnt-out candles multiply.

THERMOPYLAE

Honor to those who in their lives
are committed and guard their Thermopylae.
Never stirring from duty;
just and upright in all their deeds,
but with pity and compassion too;
generous whenever they are rich, and when
they are poor, again a little generous,
again helping as much as they are able;
always speaking the truth,
but without rancor for those who lie.

And they merit greater honor
when they foresee (and many do foresee)
that Ephialtes will finally appear,
and in the end the Medes will go through.

CHE FECE . . . IL GRAN RIFIUTO

To certain people there comes a day
when they must say the great Yes or the great No.
He who has the Yes ready within him
reveals himself at once, and saying it he crosses over

to the path of honor and his own conviction.
He who refuses does not repent. Should he be asked again,
he would say No again. And yet that No—
the right No—crushes him for the rest of his life.

THE SOULS OF OLD MEN

In their bodies wasted and aged
sit the souls of old men.
How grievous are the poor things
and how bored with the miserable life they endure.
How they tremble lest they lose it and how they dote on it
the confounded and contradictory
souls, that sit—comicotragical—
in their aged worn-out hides.

INTERRUPTION

We interrupt the work of the gods,
bustling and inexperienced beings of the moment.
In the palaces of Phthia and Eleusis
Demeter and Thetis start notable works
amid high flames and dense smoke. But
always Metaneira rushes from her royal
rooms, disheveled and terrified,
and always Peleus is fearful and interferes.

THE WINDOWS

In these darkened rooms, where I spend
oppressive days, I pace to and fro and around,
searching for the windows.—When a window
opens it will be a consolation.—
But the windows are not found, or I cannot
find them. And perhaps it is better I do not find them.
Perhaps the light will be a new tyranny.
Who knows what new things it will show?

THE TROJANS

Our efforts are the efforts of the unfortunate;
our efforts are like those of the Trojans.
We succeed somewhat; we regain confidence
somewhat; and we start once more
to have courage and high hopes.

But something always happens and stops us.
Achilles in the trench emerges before us
and with loud cries dismays us.—

Our efforts are like those of the Trojans.
We think that with resolution and daring,
we will alter the downdrag of destiny,
and we stand outside ready for battle.

But when the great crisis comes,
our daring and our resolution vanish;
our soul is agitated, paralyzed;
and we run all around the walls
seeking to save ourselves in flight.

However, our fall is certain. Above,
on the walls, the dirge has already begun.
The memories and the feelings of our own days weep.
Priam and Hecuba weep bitterly for us.

FOOTSTEPS

On an ebony bed, ornamented
with coral eagles, sound asleep, lies
Nero—unconscious, quiet and blissful,
flourishing in the vigor of the flesh
and in the splendid strength of youth.

But in the alabaster hall enclosing
the ancient shrine of the Aenobarbi
how restive are his Lares.
The small household gods tremble
and they try to hide their insignificant bodies.
For they heard a sinister clamor,
a deathly clamor ascending the stairs;
iron footsteps rattling the stairs.
And now in a faint the miserable Lares
bury themselves in the rear of the shrine;
one tumbles and stumbles over the other,
one little god falls over the other
for they understand what sort of clamor this is,
by now they already know the Furies' footsteps.

MONOTONY

One monotonous day follows another
identical monotony. The same things
will happen, they will happen again—
the same moments find us and leave us.

A month passes and ushers in another month.
One can easily guess the coming events;
they are those tedious ones of yesterday.
And the morrow ends by not resembling a morrow

WALLS

Without consideration, without pity, without shame
they have built big and high walls around me.

And now I sit here despairing.
I think of nothing else: this fate gnaws at my mind;

for I had many things to do outside.
Ah why didn't I observe them when they were building the walls?

But I never heard the noise or the sound of the builders.
Imperceptibly they shut me out of the world.

EXPECTING THE BARBARIANS

What are we waiting for, assembled in the public square?

The barbarians are to arrive today.

Why such inaction in the Senate?
Why do the Senators sit and pass no laws?

Because the barbarians are to arrive today.
What further laws can the Senators pass?
When the barbarians come they will make the laws.

Why did our emperor wake up so early,
and sits at the principal gate of the city,
on the throne, in state, wearing his crown?

Because the barbarians are to arrive today.
And the emperor waits to receive
their chief. Indeed he has prepared
to give him a scroll. Therein he engraved
many titles and names of honor.

Why have our two consuls and the praetors come out
today in their red, embroidered togas;
why do they wear amethyst-studded bracelets,
and rings with brilliant glittering emeralds;
why are they carrying costly canes today,
superbly carved with silver and gold?

Because the barbarians are to arrive today,
and such things dazzle the barbarians.

Why don't the worthy orators come as usual
to make their speeches, to have their say?

Because the barbarians are to arrive today;
and they get bored with eloquence and orations.

Why this sudden unrest and confusion?
(How solemn their faces have become.)
Why are the streets and squares clearing quickly,
and all return to their homes, so deep in thought?

Because night is here but the barbarians have not come.
Some people arrived from the frontiers,
and they said that there are no longer any barbarians.

And now what shall become of us without any barbarians?
Those people were a kind of solution.

INFIDELITY

Though many things are praised in Homer, there is one thing we do not praise . . . in Aeschylus where Thetis says that Apollo singing at her wedding prophesied the good fortune of her offspring, granted them a life free of illness, long years of life. Then he said that my fate would be blessed by the gods, and he sang paeans wishing me joy. And I hoped to find true these divine words of Phoebus, surpassing all in the art of prophecy. But he himself who sang . . . he himself slew my son.
PLATO's *Republic*, B

At the nuptial banquet of Thetis and Peleus
Apollo rose from the sumptuous marriage
table, and gave the newlyweds his divine blessing
for the offspring that would be born of their union.
He said, "No sickness shall ever touch him and he
shall have a long, long life."—When he spoke these words,
Thetis rejoiced beyond measure, for the words
of Apollo who knew all about prophecies
seemed to her a guarantee for the life of her son.
And through the years when Achilles was growing up
and his fine looks were the glory of Thessaly,
Thetis remembered the words of the god.
But one day old men arrived with news
and they told of the slaying of Achilles at Troy.
And Thetis tore off her purple garments,
and she kept on tearing off and casting upon
the ground her bracelets and rings.
And in her lamentation she recalled the past;
and she asked what the wise Apollo was doing,
where was the poet wandering who speaks
so divinely at feasts, where was the prophet roaming
when they were slaying her son in the prime of his youth.
And the old men answered her that Apollo
himself had gone down to Troy,
and with the Trojans he had slain Achilles.

THE FUNERAL OF SARPEDON

Zeus is deeply grieved. Patroclus
has slain Sarpedon; and now the son of Menoetius
and the Achaeans rush headlong
to seize and shame his body.

But Zeus does not countenance these things.
His dearly loved child—whom he had left
to perish; for such was the Law—
at least he will honor him in death.
And see, he sends Phoebus down to the plain
with instructions for the care of the body.

Phoebus lifts up the corpse of the hero with respect
and in sorrow and carries it to the river.
He washes him of all the dust and the blood;
binds the frightening wounds, not leaving
a single trace to show; pours ambrosial
perfumes over him; dresses him
in magnificent Olympian robes.
He whitens his skin; and with a pearl-studded comb
he combs out his jet-black hair.
He straightens and lays out his beautiful limbs.

Now he resembles a young king charioteer—
in his twenty-fifth or twenty-sixth year—
taking his rest after having won,
with a chariot all of gold and with swiftest steeds,
the prize in a famous contest.

So when Phoebus had completed
his mission, he summoned his two brothers
Sleep and Death, commanding them
to take the body to Lycia, the rich land.

And toward that rich land, toward Lycia,
these two brothers Sleep and Death
went on foot, and when they at last arrived
at the gate of the royal house
they delivered the glorious body,
and then returned to their other cares and tasks.

And when they received it there, in the house,
the sad burial started with processions,
and honors and dirges and lavish libations
from holy chalices and with all things meet;
and then skilled laborers from the city,
and illustrious workmen in stone
came and built the tomb and the monument.

DIONYSUS AND HIS CREW

Damon the artisan (there is no one more
capable in the Peloponnese) carves the crew
of Dionysus in Parian marble.
At the head, the God in sublime glory,
with power in his walk.
Ácratos follows him. Beside Ácratos,
Méthe pours the wine for the Satyrs
out of an ivy-wreathed amphora.
Near them is Hedýoinos, the soft one,
his eyes half-shut, heavy with sleep.
Behind them come the singers
Mólpos and Hedymelés, and Cómus who holds
the revered torch of the procession and
never lets it go out; and most diffident Teleté.—
These Damon carves. And along with these,
every so often his mind deliberates
on his fee from the king of Syracuse,
three talents, a goodly sum.
When this is added to the rest of his money,
then he can live in style, grandly, like a man of means,
and he will be able to go into politics—joy!—
he too in the senate, he too in the market place.

THE HORSES OF ACHILLES

When they saw that Patroclus was slain,
who had been so stalwart, and strong, and young,
the horses of Achilles started to weep;
their immortal nature was indignant
at the sight of this work of death.
They would shake their heads and toss their manes,
stamp the ground with their feet, and mourn
Patroclus who they realized was lifeless—undone—
worthless flesh now—his spirit lost—
defenseless—without breath—
returned from life to the great Nothing.

Zeus saw the tears of the immortal horses
and grew sad. "At the wedding of Peleus,"
he said, "I should not have acted so thoughtlessly;
it would have been better my hapless horses
if we had not given you! What are you doing down there,
among woebegone humanity, the plaything of fate?
You for whom neither death nor old age lie in wait,
you are harassed by transitory calamities.
Men have implicated you in their troubles."—Yet the two
noble animals went on shedding their tears
for the never-ending calamity of death.

HE IS THE MAN

An unknown—a stranger in Antioch—an Edessan
writes and writes. And see, the last lay
is finally done. That makes eighty-three

poems in all. But so much writing,
so much versifying, have fatigued the poet,
and so much strain from Greek phrase-making,
and now every little thing presses heavily upon him.—

But one thought instantly takes him out of
his despondency—the excellent He Is the Man,
that Lucian at another time heard in his sleep.

KING DEMETRIUS

Not like a king, but like an actor,
instead of his royal robe, he put on a
gray cloak and stealthily departed.
PLUTARCH, "Life of Demetrius."

When the Macedonians abandoned him,
and proved that they prefer Pyrrhus,
King Demetrius (he had a great soul)
did not—so they stated—behave
in the least like a king. He went
and took off his robes of gold,
and cast off his purple shoes.
He dressed hurriedly
in simple clothes and went off.
Behaving like an actor
who when the performance is over
changes his clothes and departs.

THE CITY

You said, "I will go to another land, I will go to another sea.
Another city will be found, a better one than this.
Every effort of mine is a condemnation of fate;
and my heart is—like a corpse—buried.
How long will my mind remain in this wasteland.
Wherever I turn my eyes, wherever I may look
I see black ruins of my life here,
where I spent so many years destroying and wasting."

You will find no new lands, you will find no other seas.
The city will follow you. You will roam the same
streets. And you will age in the same neighborhoods;
and you will grow gray in these same houses.
Always you will arrive in this city. Do not hope for any other—
There is no ship for you, there is no road.
As you have destroyed your life here
in this little corner, you have ruined it in the entire world.

SATRAPY

What a misfortune, though you are made
for fine and important works
this unjust fate of yours always
denies you encouragement and success;
that base customs should block you;
and pettiness and indifference.
And how frightful the day when you yield
(the day when you give up and yield)
and you leave on foot for Susa,
and you go to the monarch Artaxerxes
who graciously gives you a place in his court,
and offers you satrapies and such.
And you accept with despair
these things you do not want.
Your soul seeks other things, weeps for other things;
the praise of the people and the Sophists,
the hard-won, invaluable Well Done;
the Agora, the Theater, and the Laurels.
How can Artaxerxes give you these?
Where will you find these in a satrapy?
And without these, what life can you live?

THE IDES OF MARCH

Fear grandeurs, O my soul.
And if you cannot triumph over your
ambitions, pursue them with hesitation
and precaution. And the more you go forward,
the more searching, attentive you must be.

And when you reach your peak, Caesar at last;
when you take on the form of a famous man,
then above all take heed as you go out on the street,
a man of authority conspicuous with your followers,
if by chance out of the mob some Artemidorus
should approach you, who brings you a letter,
and hastily says, "Read this at once,
it contains grave matters of concern to you,"
do not fail to stop; do not fail to put off
all talk or work; do not fail to turn away
the various people who salute you and kneel before you
(you can see them later); let even the Senate
itself wait, and immediately get to know
the grave writings of Artemidorus.

THE GOD FORSAKES ANTONY

When suddenly at the midnight hour
an invisible troupe is heard passing
with exquisite music, with shouts—
do not mourn in vain your fortune failing you now,
your works that have failed, the plans of your life
that have all turned out to be illusions.
As if long prepared for this, as if courageous,
bid her farewell, the Alexandria that is leaving.
Above all do not be fooled, do not tell yourself
it was only a dream, that your ears deceived you;
do not stoop to such vain hopes.
As if long prepared for this, as if courageous,
as it becomes you who are worthy of such a city;
approach the window with firm step,
and listen with emotion, but not
with the entreaties and complaints of the coward,
as a last enjoyment listen to the sounds,
the exquisite instruments of the mystical troupe,
and bid her farewell, the Alexandria you are losing.

FINALITIES

Plunged in fear and suspicions,
with agitated mind and frightened eyes,
we melt, and plan how to act
in order to avoid the certain
danger so frightfully menacing us.
And yet we err, it is not in our paths;
the messages were false alarms,
(or else we did not hear, or fully understand them).
Another catastrophe, that we never imagined,
suddenly, torrentially falls upon us,
and unprepared—there is no more time—carries us off.

IONIAN SONG

Though we have broken their statues,
though we have driven them out of their temples,
the gods did not die because of this at all.
O Ionian land, it is you they still love,
it is you their souls still remember.
When the August morning dawns upon you
a vigor from their life moves through your air;
and at times a figure of ethereal youth,
indistinct, in rapid stride,
crosses over your hills.

SCULPTOR OF TYANA

As you have probably heard, I am no novice.
A good deal of stone passes through my hands.
And in my native land, Tyana, they know
me well; and here too senators have ordered
numerous statues from me.

And let me show you
some of them right now. Look closely at this Rhea:
venerable, full of forbearance, quite ancient.
Look closely at Pompey. Marius,
Aemilius Paulus, Scipio Africanus.
Faithful likenesses, as good as I could make them.
Patroclus (I will retouch him a little).
Near that yellowish marble
those pieces over there, is Caesarion.

And now for some time I have been busy
making a Poseidon. I am studying
the horses in particular, how to mold them.
They must be made so light that
their bodies, their feet, must clearly show
they do not tread the earth, but run on the sea.

But here is the work that I love best,
that I have toiled over with feeling and with the greatest care;
him, on a warm day of summer,
when my mind was soaring toward the ideal,
I dreamt of him, of this young Hermes here.

PERILOUS THINGS

Said Myrtias (a Syrian student
in Alexandria; in the reign of
Augustus Constans and Augustus Constantius;
in part a pagan and in part a christian),
"Fortified by theory and by study,
I shall not fear my passions like a coward.
I shall yield my body to sensual delights,
to enjoyments that one dreams about,
to the most audacious amorous desires,
to the wanton impulses of my blood, without
a single fear, for whenever I wish—
and I shall have the will, fortified
as I shall be by theory and by study—
at moments of crisis, I shall find again
my spirit, as before, ascetic."

THE GLORY OF THE PTOLEMIES

I am the son of Lagus, king. The absolute possessor
(with my power and my wealth) of voluptuous delight.
No Macedonian, or barbarian, can be found
my equal, or even to compare with me. The son of Seleucus
is ludicrous with his vulgar luxury.
But if you want more, see, these too are clear.
The city—the teacher, summit of panhellenism,
in the word, in every art, the wisest.

ITHACA

When you start on your journey to Ithaca,
then pray that the road is long,
full of adventure, full of knowledge.
Do not fear the Lestrygonians
and the Cyclopes and the angry Poseidon.
You will never meet such as these on your path,
if your thoughts remain lofty, if a fine
emotion touches your body and your spirit.
You will never meet the Lestrygonians,
the Cyclopes and the fierce Poseidon,
if you do not carry them within your soul,
if your soul does not raise them up before you.

Then pray that the road is long.
That the summer mornings are many,
that you will enter ports seen for the first time
with such pleasure, with such joy!
Stop at Phoenician markets,
and purchase fine merchandise,
mother-of-pearl and corals, amber and ebony,
and pleasurable perfumes of all kinds,
buy as many pleasurable perfumes as you can;
visit hosts of Egyptian cities,
to learn and learn from those who have knowledge.

Always keep Ithaca fixed in your mind.
To arrive there is your ultimate goal.
But do not hurry the voyage at all.
It is better to let it last for long years;
and even to anchor at the isle when you are old,
rich with all that you have gained on the way,
not expecting that Ithaca will offer you riches.

Ithaca has given you the beautiful voyage.

Without her you would never have taken the road.
But she has nothing more to give you.

And if you find her poor, Ithaca has not defrauded you.
With the great wisdom you have gained, with so much experience,
you must surely have understood by then what Ithacas mean.

HEROD OF ATTICA

Ah, what a glory this is, of Herod of Attica!

Alexander of Seleucia, one of our fine sophists,
arriving at Athens to speak,
finds the city deserted, because Herod
was in the country. And all the young men
had followed him there to hear him.
So Alexander the Sophist
writes Herod a letter,
and begs him to send the Greeks.
But the shrewd Herod answers at once,
"I too am coming, along with the Greeks."—

How many lads in Alexandria now,
in Antioch, or in Beirut
(tomorrow's orators that hellenism trains),
when they gather at their choice tables
where sometimes the talk is of splendid sophistries,
and sometimes of their exquisite love affairs,
suddenly distracted, they become silent.
They leave the glasses near them untouched,
while they contemplate Herod's good fortune—
what other sophist ever achieved as much?—
Just as he wishes, just as he does
the Greeks (the Greeks!) follow him,
not to judge or to discuss,
not even to choose any more, only to follow.

PHILHELLENE

See that the engraving is artistic.
The expression serious and stately.
The crown had better be rather narrow;
I do not like those broad Parthian ones.
The inscription, as usual, in Greek;
not exaggerated, not pompous—
lest the proconsul who is always poking about
and reporting to Rome misconstrue it—
but nonetheless of course dignified.
Something very special on the other side;
some good-looking discus-thrower in his prime.
Above all I charge you to see to it
(Sithaspes, in God's name, let this not be forgotten)
that after the words King and Savior,
there be engraved in elegant letters, Philhellene.
Now don't try your clever sallies on me,
your "Where are the Greeks?" and "Where is anything Greek
behind Zagros here, beyond Phraata?"
Since so many others more barbarous than we
write it, we too shall write it.
And finally do not forget that at times
sophists from Syria visit us,
and versifiers, and other wiseacres.
So we are not un-Greek, I reckon.

ALEXANDRIAN KINGS

The Alexandrians are gathered together
to see Cleopatra's children,
Caesarion and his little brothers,
Alexander and Ptolemy, whom they lead forth
for the first time to the Stadium,
there to proclaim them kings,
amid the brilliant procession of soldiers.

Alexander—they named him king
of Armenia, Media, and the Parthians.
Ptolemy—they named him king
of Cilicia, Syria, and Phoenicia.
Caesarion stood more to the front,
dressed in rose-colored silk,
on his breast a bouquet of hyacinths,
his belt a double row of sapphires and amethysts,
his shoes tied with white ribbons
embroidered with rose-colored pearls.
Him they named oftener than the younger ones,
him they named King of Kings.

The Alexandrians surely perceived
that all these were theatrical words.

But the day was warm and poetic,
the sky a lucid, azure blue,
the Alexandria Stadium
a triumphant achievement of art,
the superb splendor of the courtiers,
Caesarion all grace and beauty
(Cleopatra's sons, blood of the Lagidae)
and so the Alexandrians rushed to the ceremony,
and they grew enthusiastic, and they cheered
in Greek and in Egyptian and some in Hebrew,

enchanted by the gorgeous spectacle—
knowing full well the worth of all these,
what hollow words these kingships were.

IN CHURCH

I love the church—its hexapteriga,
the silver of its sacred vessels, its candlesticks,
the lights, its icons, its pulpit.

When I enter a church of the Greeks,
with its fragrances of incense,
with its voices and liturgical choirs,
the stately presence of the priests
and the solemn rhythm of each of their movements—
most resplendent in the adornment of their vestments
my mind goes to the high honors of our race,
to the glory of our Byzantine tradition.

RETURN

Return often and take me,
beloved sensation, return and take me—
when the memory of the body awakens,
and old desire again runs through the blood;
when the lips and the skin remember,
and the hands feel as if they touch again.

Return often and take me at night,
when the lips and the skin remember . . .

AS MUCH AS YOU CAN

And if you cannot make your life as you want it,
at least try this
as much as you can: do not disgrace it
in the crowding contact with the world,
in the many movements and all the talk.

Do not disgrace it by taking it,
dragging it around often and exposing it
to the daily folly
of relationships and associations,
till it becomes like an alien burdensome life.

VERY SELDOM

He is an old man. Worn out and stooped,
maimed by the years, and by abuses,
with slow step he crosses the narrow street.
And yet as he enters his door to hide
his wretchedness and his old age, he meditates
on the share he still has of youth.

Now young people recite his verses.
In their lively eyes his fancies pass.
Their sound, voluptuous minds,
their shapely, firm flesh
are stirred by his expression of beauty.

I WENT

I did not tether myself. I let go entirely and went,
I went into the luminous night,
to those pleasures that were half real,
and half wheeling in my brain.
And I drank of potent wines, as only the
valiant of voluptuousness drink.

OF THE SHOP

He wrapped them carefully, tidily
in costly green silk.

Roses of ruby, and lilies of pearl, and violets
of amethyst. As he himself estimates them, as he

wanted them, to him they look beautiful; not as he saw them
in nature or studied them. He will leave them in the safe,

a sample of his intrepid and skillful craft.
When a customer walks into the shop,

he takes from the cases other wares to sell—superb jewels—
bracelets, chains, necklaces, and rings.

THE GRAVE OF THE GRAMMARIAN LYSIAS

Very close to you, as you enter on the right, in the Beirut
library, we buried the sage Lysias,
the grammarian. The spot is beautifully right.
We placed him near those things of his that he perhaps
remembers even there—scholia, texts, grammars,
scriptures, numerous commentaries in tomes on hellenisms.
This way, his grave will also be seen and honored
by us, when we pass among the books.

FAR OFF

I should like to relate this memory . . .
but it is so faded now . . . scarcely anything is left—
because it lies far off, in the years of my early manhood.

A skin as if made of jasmine . . .
that night in August—was it August?—that night . . .
I can just barely remember the eyes; they were, I think, blue . . .
Ah yes, blue; a sapphire blue.

THE GRAVE OF EURION

In this ingenious tomb,
entirely of syenite stone,
that so many violets, so many lilies cover,
the handsome Eurion lies buried.
An Alexandrian boy, twenty-five years of age.
On his father's side, of an old stock of Macedonians;
of a line of magistrates on his mother's side.
He was a student of Aristocleitus in philosophy,
of Paros in rhetoric. In Thebes he studied
sacred letters. He wrote a history
of the province of Arsinoe. That at least will remain.
But we have lost the most precious—his form,
that was an Apollonian vision.

CHANDELIER

In a room bare and small, only the four walls
covered with solid green strips of cloth,
a beautiful chandelier burns and blazes;
and in each of its flames kindles
a prurient passion, a prurient urge.

Within the small room shining brightly,
lit by the strong flame of the chandelier,
this is no ordinary light that shines.
The sensual delight of this warmth
is not made for timorous bodies.

THEODOTUS

If you are truly one of the select few,
watch how you acquire your power.
However much you are glorified, however much
the cities in Italy and in Thessaly
acclaim your achievements,
however many decrees in your honor
your admirers may have issued in Rome,
neither your joy nor your triumph will last,
nor will you feel like a superior—what do you mean superior?—man
when in Alexandria, Theodotus brings you,
upon a bloodstained tray,
the head of the wretched Pompey.

And do not rely on the fact that in your life,
circumscribed, regulated, and prosaic,
there are no such spectacular and terrifying things.
Perhaps at this very hour, Theodotus is entering
the well-appointed house of one of your neighbors—
invisible, bodiless—
carrying such a hideous head.

BUT WISE MEN PERCEIVE APPROACHING THINGS

For the gods perceive future events, men what is
happening now, but wise men approaching things.
PHILOSTRATUS, *Life of Apollonius of Tyana*, viii, 7

People know what is happening now.
The gods know things of the future,
the entire and sole possessors of all the lights.
Of the things of the future, wise men perceive
approaching events. At times

during hours of serious meditations
their hearing is disturbed. The mysterious clamor
of approaching events reaches them.
And they listen with reverence. Although outside
on the street, the peoples hear nothing at all.

MORNING SEA

Let me stand here. Let me also look at nature a while.
The shore of the morning sea and the cloudless
sky brilliant blue and yellow
all illuminated lovely and large.

Let me stand here. Let me delude myself that I see these things
(I really did see them a moment when I first stopped);
and not that here too I see my fantasies,
my memories, my visions of sensual delight.

AT THE CAFÉ ENTRANCE

Something they said beside me directed
my attention toward the café entrance.
And I saw the beautiful body that looked
as if Eros had made it from his consummate experience—
joyfully modeling its symmetrical limbs;
heightening sculpturally its stature;
modeling the face with emotion
and imparting by the touch of his hands
a feeling on the brow, on the eyes, on the lips.

OROPHERNES

He who here upon the tetradrachm
appears to have a smiling face,
the handsome, delicate face,
he is Orophernes, son of Ariarathes.

As a child they cast him out of Cappadocia,
out of the great paternal palace,
and they sent him away to grow up
in Ionia, to be forgotten among strangers.

O those rapturous Ionian nights
when dauntless, and entirely *à la grecque*
he came to know the fullness of pleasure.
In his heart, always an Asiatic;
but in his manners and in his speech Greek,
adorned in turquoise, in Greek dress,
his body scented with attar of jasmine,
and of the handsome Ionian boys,
he is the handsomest, the most ideal.

Then when the Syrians entered
Cappadocia, and made him king,
he threw himself into his kingship
to enjoy himself daily in a new way,
to gather rapaciously gold and silver,
and to rejoice and to boast of the piles
of riches he saw glittering before him.
As for care of country, or for governing—
he didn't even know what went on around him.

The Cappadocians quickly removed him;
and he ended up in Syria, in the palace
of Demetrius, pleasuring and idling.

One day, however, unaccustomed thoughts
interrupted his great laziness;
he recalled that by his mother Antiochida,
and by that aged lady Stratonice,
he too was descended from the crown of Syria,
and was himself almost a Seleucid.
For a while he came out of his lust and drunkenness,
and ineptly, and half dazed
he sought to start an intrigue,
to do something, to plan something,
and he failed miserably and fell into contempt.

His end must have been written somewhere and lost;
or perhaps history passed over it,
and, justifiably, it did not deign
to record so trifling a matter.

He who here upon this tetradrachm
has left a charm of his exquisite youth,
a light from his poetic beauty,
an aesthetic memory of an Ionian boy,
he is Orophernes, son of Ariarathes.

HE SWEARS

Every so often he swears to start a finer life.
But when night comes with its own counsels,
its compromises, and its promises;
but when night comes with its own vigor
of the body, craving and seeking, he returns,
forlorn, to the same fatal joy.

ON PAINTING

I attend to my work and I love it.
But today the languor of composition disheartens me.
The day has affected me. Its face
is deepening dark. It continues to blow and rain.
I would sooner see than speak.
In this painting now, I am looking at
a beautiful lad who is stretched out
near the fountain, probably worn out from running.
What a beautiful child; what a divine noon
has now overtaken him to lull him to sleep.—
I sit and look so for a long time.
And again it is in art that I rest from its toil.

ONE NIGHT

The room was poor and squalid,
hidden above the dubious tavern.
From the window you could see the alley
filthy and narrow. From below
came the voices of some workmen
playing cards and carousing.

And there on the much-used, lowly bed
I had the body of love, I had the lips,
the voluptuous and rosy lips of ecstasy—
rosy lips of such ecstasy, that even now
as I write, after so many years!
in my solitary house, I am drunk again.

THE BATTLE OF MAGNESIA

He lost his old spirit, his courage.
His tired body, almost sick,

will be his main concern. And the rest of his
life will be spent free of care. This at least

Philip maintains. Tonight he plays at dice;
he is in a mood for amusement. Set many roses

on the table. What if Antiochus was destroyed
in Magnesia? They say complete carnage

fell on the ranks of his brilliant army.
Perhaps they exaggerated; it cannot all be true.

God grant it. For though our enemy, they were of one race.
But one "God grant it" is enough. Perhaps even too much.

Philip of course will not postpone the feast.
However long his life's tedium has lasted,

one good thing he retains, his memory shows no lapse.
He recalls how much they wept in Syria, what sort of sorrow

they felt, when their Mother Macedonia became dirt.—
Let the dinner start! Slaves, the flutes, the torches.

MANUEL COMNENUS

The King Kyr Manuel Comnenus
one melancholy day in September
felt that death was near. The court
astrologers (the paid ones) babbled
that he would live for many more years.
But while they were discoursing,
he remembered old hallowed customs,
and from the cells of the monks he bids
them bring ecclesiastical robes,
and he wears them, and rejoices that he presents
the modest mien of a priest or a monk.

All are lucky who believe
and like the King Kyr Manuel end their days
most modestly dressed in their faith.

THE DISPLEASURE OF THE SON OF SELEUCUS

Demetrius, son of Seleucus, was displeased
to learn that a Ptolemy
had arrived in Italy in such a state.
With only three or four slaves;
poorly dressed and on foot. From now on
this will reduce the people of their race to objects of irony
and playthings in Rome. That at bottom
they have become a sort of servant of the Romans
the son of Seleucus knows; that the Romans
bestow and take back their thrones
arbitrarily, as they please, he knows.
But at least in their appearance
let them preserve something of their majesty;
let them not forget that they are still kings,
that they are still (alas!) called kings.

This is why Demetrius, the son of Seleucus
is disturbed; and at once he offered Ptolemy
all purple robes, a sparkling crown,
costly jewels, numerous servants
and followers, his most precious steeds,
that he might present himself properly in Rome,
as an Alexandrian Greek monarch.

But the son of Lagus, who had come to beg,
knew what he was after and he refused them all;
he had no need whatever of these luxuries.
Poorly dressed, humble, he entered Rome,
and lodged at the house of a little artisan.
And then he presented himself to the Senate
as a woebegone creature and as a pauper,
so that he might beg with greater success.

ON THE STREET

His compassionate face, slightly wan;
his chestnut eyes, as if ringed;
he is twenty-five years old, but looks more like twenty;
with something artistic in his dress,
—a touch of color in his tie, a bit of shape to his collar—
he walks aimlessly on the street,
as if hypnotized still by the deviate sensual delight,
by the so deviate sensual delight he has enjoyed.

WHEN THEY ARE ROUSED

Try to guard them, poet,
however few there are that can be kept.
The visions of your loving.
Set them, half hidden, in your phrases.
Try to sustain them, poet,
when they are roused in your brain
at night, or in the glare of noon.

BEFORE THE STATUE OF ENDYMION

I arrive in Latmus from Miletus
in a white chariot drawn by four
snow-white, silver-ornamented mules. For the
sacred rites—sacrifices and libations—to Endymion.
I sailed from Alexandria in a purple trireme.—
Look at the statue. Now ecstatic I gaze
at Endymion's illustrious beauty.
My slaves empty baskets of jasmine; and auspicious
applause awakens pleasure of ancient days.

GRAY

Looking at a half-gray opal
I remembered two beautiful gray eyes
I had seen; it must have been twenty years ago . . .

. . . .

For a month we loved each other.
Then he went away, I believe to Smyrna,
to work there, and we never saw each other after that.

The gray eyes—if he is alive—must have grown ugly;
the handsome face must have spoiled.

Dear Memory, preserve them as they used to be.
And, Memory, bring back to me tonight all that you can,
of this love of mine, all that you can.

IN A TOWN OF OSROENE

Yesterday about midnight they brought home
our friend Rhemon, wounded in a tavern brawl.
Through the window which we left wide open,
the moon lighted his handsome body on the bed.
We are an assortment here; Syrians, Greeks, Armenians, Medes.
Rhemon is one of these too. But yesterday
as the moon illumined his amorous face,
our minds went back to Plato's Charmides.

ONE OF THEIR GODS

When one of Them passed through Seleucia's
market place, toward the hour when night comes on,
in the guise of a tall and perfectly handsome youth,
with the joy of incorruptibility in his eyes,
with his black, heavily perfumed hair,
the passers-by would stare at him
and one would ask the other if he knew him,
if he were a Greek of Syria or a stranger. But
several who watched with greater attention
understood and would stand aside;
and as he vanished under the arcades,
among the shadows and among the evening lights,
heading toward the district which comes alive
only at night, with orgies and debauchery,
and every sort of drunkenness and lust,
they would wonder which of Them he might be,
and for what questionable enjoyment
he had descended to the streets of Seleucia
from those Adored, Most Venerable Halls.

TOMB OF IASES

I, Iases, lie here. The young man
renowned for beauty, of this great city.
The very wise admired me; and also the shallow
common people. I was pleased alike by both.

But by dint of the world's having me be a Narcissus and Hermes,
dissipation ravaged me, killed me. Traveler,
if you are an Alexandrian, you will not condemn. You know
the rushing torrent of our life; what ardor it has; what supreme
pleasure.

PASSAGE

Those things that a student timidly imagines are open
plainly before him. And he roams, and spends sleepless nights,
and is led astray. And since (for our art) it is right,
voluptuousness enjoys
his new, ardent blood. Deviate erotic drunkenness
overcomes him; and his young limbs
yield to it.
            And so a simple lad
becomes worthy of our attention, and through the High
World of Poetry for a moment he too passes—
the sensitive lad with his blood new and ardent.

IN THE EVENING

Anyway those things would not have lasted long. The experience
of the years shows it to me. But Destiny arrived
in some haste and stopped them.
The beautiful life was brief.
But how potent were the perfumes,
on how splendid a bed we lay,
to what sensual delight we gave our bodies.

An echo of the days of pleasure,
an echo of the days drew near me,
a little of the fire of the youth of both of us;
again I took in my hands a letter,
and I read and reread till the light was gone.

And melancholy, I came out on the balcony—
came out to change my thoughts at least by looking at
a little of the city that I loved,
a little movement on the street, and in the shops.

FOR AMMONIS, WHO DIED AT 29 IN 610

Raphael, they are asking you to compose
a few verses as an epitaph for the poet Ammonis.
Something with particular taste and polish. You will be able,
you are just the man, to write fittingly
of the poet Ammonis, who was ours.

Naturally you will speak of his poems—
but speak of his beauty too,
of his delicate beauty that we loved.

Your Greek is always beautiful and musical.
But now we desire all your mastery.
Our sorrow and love pass into a foreign tongue.
Pour your Egyptian feeling into a foreign tongue.

Raphael, your verses should be written so
that they will have, you know, something in them of our life,
so that the rhythm and each phrase will show
that an Alexandrian is writing of an Alexandrian.

IN THE MONTH OF ATHYR

With difficulty I read   on the ancient stone
"LO(RD) JESUS CHRIST."   I make out a "SO(U)L."
"IN THE MON(TH) OF ATHYR."   "LEUCIU(S) FELL A(SL)EEP."
Where they mention age   "HE LI(VE)D . . . YEARS."
The Kappa Zeta shows   that he fell asleep young.
Among the worn-away pieces   I see "HI(M) . . . ALEXANDRIAN."
Then there are three lines   that are quite mutilated;
but I make out a few words—   as "OUR TE(A)RS," "SORROW,"
then again "TEARS,"   and "W(E) HIS (F)RIENDS MOURN."
It seems to me that Leucius   must have been dearly beloved.
In the month of Athyr   Leucius fell asleep.

THE TOMB OF IGNATIUS

Here I am not that Cleon celebrated
in Alexandria (where it is hard to astonish them)
for my magnificent houses, for the gardens,
for my horses and for my chariots,
for the jewels and silks that I wore.
God forbid; here I am not that Cleon;
let his twenty-eight years be erased.
I am Ignatius, a reader, who came to my self
quite late; but I lived so for ten months
happy in the serenity and security of Christ.

SO MUCH I GAZED

So much I gazed on beauty,
my vision is alive with it.

Contours of the body. Red lips. Voluptuous limbs.
Hair as if taken from Greek statues;
always beautiful, even when uncombed,
and it falls, a little, over the white temples.
Faces of love, exactly as my poetry
desired them . . . in the nights of my young manhood,
deep in my nights, in secret, encountered . . .

DAYS OF 1903

I never found them again—those things so speedily lost . . .
the poetic eyes, the pallid face . . . .
in the dusk of the road. . . .

I never found them again—those quite haphazardly acquired,
that I gave up so lightly;
and that later in agony I craved.
The poetic eyes, the pallid face,
I never found those lips again.

THE TOBACCO-SHOP WINDOW

They stood among many others
near a lighted tobacco-shop window.
Their glances chanced to meet,
and they timidly, haltingly expressed
the deviate desire of their flesh.
Then, a few steps uneasily taken on the sidewalk—
until they smiled, and gently nodded.

And after that the closed carriage . . .
the carnal closeness of their bodies;
the clasped hands, the met lips.

SENSUAL DELIGHT

The joy and essence of my life is the memory of the hours
when I found and sustained sensual delight as I desired it.
The joy and essence of my life for me, who abhorred
every enjoyment of routine loves.

CAESARION

Partly to verify an epoch,
partly also to pass the time,
last night I picked up a collection
of Ptolemaic inscriptions to read.
The plentiful praises and flatteries
suit everyone. Everyone is brilliant,
glorious, mighty, beneficent;
each enterprise of theirs the wisest.
If you talk of the women of that breed, they too,
all the Berenices and Cleopatras, are admirable.

When I had managed to verify the epoch
I would have put the book aside had not a small,
meaningless mention of the king Caesarion
immediately attracted my attention.

Ah, see, you came with your vague
fascination. In history only a few
lines are found about you,
and so I molded you more freely in my mind.
I molded you handsome and full of sentiment.
My art gives your features
a dreamy compassionate beauty.
And so fully did I vision you,
that late last night as my lamp
was going out—I deliberately let it go out—
I thought I saw you enter my room,
you seemed to stand before me as you must have been
in vanquished Alexandria,
wan and weary, idealistic in your sorrow,
still hoping that they would pity you,
the wicked—who murmured "Too many Caesars."

IN HARBOR

A young man, twenty-eight years of age, Emes arrived
at this little Syrian harbor on a tenion vessel
with the intention of learning to be a perfume seller.
But during the voyage he fell ill; and as soon
as he disembarked, he died. His burial, the very poorest,
took place here. A few hours before he died,
he murmured something about "home," about "very old parents."
But who they were nobody knew,
nor which his country in the vast panhellenic world.
It is better so. For in this way, though
he lies dead in this little harbor,
his parents will always go on hoping he is alive.

BODY, REMEMBER . . .

Body, remember not only how much you were loved,
not only the beds on which you lay,
but also those desires for you
that glowed plainly in the eyes,
and trembled in the voice—and some
chance obstacle made futile.
Now that all of them belong to the past,
it almost seems as if you had yielded
to those desires—how they glowed,
remember, in the eyes gazing at you;
how they trembled in the voice, for you, remember, body.

THE TOMB OF LÁNES

The Lánes that you loved is not here, Marcus,
in the tomb, where you come and weep and stay for hours on end.
The Lánes you loved you have much closer to you
at home, when you shut yourself in and gaze at his picture
which has somehow preserved whatever was worthy in him,
which has somehow preserved whatever you loved.

Remember, Marcus, the time you brought the famous
Cyrenian painter from the palace of the proconsul,
and as soon as he set eyes on your friend
with what artistic cunning he wished to persuade you
that he simply had to do him as Hyacinth
(in this way his painting would be more celebrated).

But your Lánes would not lend his beauty so;
and firmly opposing, he told him not to present him
as Hyacinth at all, nor as anyone else
but as Lánes, son of Rhametichus, of Alexandria.

NERO'S TERM

Nero was not alarmed when he heard
the prophecy of the Delphic Oracle.
"Let him fear the seventy-three years."
There was still ample time to enjoy himself.
He is thirty years old. The term
the god allots to him is quite sufficient
for him to prepare for perils to come.

Now he will return to Rome slightly fatigued,
but delightfully fatigued from this journey,
which consisted entirely of days of pleasure
at the theaters, the gardens, the athletic fields . . .
evenings spent in the cities of Greece . . .
Ah the voluptuous delight of nude bodies, above all . . .

These things Nero thought. And in Spain Galba
secretly assembles and drills his army,
the old man of seventy-three.

THE NEXT TABLE

He must be scarcely twenty-two years old.
And yet I am certain that nearly as many
years ago, I enjoyed the very same body.

It isn't at all infatuation of love.
I entered the casino only a little while ago;
I didn't even have time to drink much.
I have enjoyed the same body.

If I can't recall where—one lapse of memory means nothing.

Ah see, now that he is sitting down at the next table
I know every movement he makes—and beneath his clothes,
once more I see the beloved bare limbs.

UNDERSTANDING

The years of my young manhood, my sensual life—
how plainly I see their meaning now.

What needless repentances, how futile . . .

But I did not grasp their meaning then.

Deep in the dissolute life of my young manhood
the designs of my poetry took shape,
the scope of my art was being plotted.

This is why even my repentances were never stable.
And my resolutions to restrain myself, to change,
lasted for two weeks at the very most.

ENVOYS FROM ALEXANDRIA

They had not seen, for ages, such lovely gifts in Delphi
as these which had been sent by the two brothers,
the two rival Ptolemaian Kings. After they had received
the gifts, however, the priests were uneasy about the oracle.
They will need all their experience to compose with astuteness,
which of the two, which of such two will be displeased.
And they sit in council in secret at night
and discuss the family affairs of the Lagidae.

But see, the envoys have come back. They are saying farewell.
They are returning to Alexandria, they say. They do not seek
any oracle whatever. And the priests hear this with joy
(it is understood they keep the remarkable gifts),
but they are also bewildered in the extreme,
not understanding what this sudden indifference means.
For they are unaware that yesterday grave news reached the envoys.
The oracle was pronounced in Rome; the division took place there.

SINCE NINE O'CLOCK—

Half past twelve. The time has passed quickly
since nine o'clock when I lit the lamp,
and sat down here. I sat without reading,
and without speaking. With whom could I speak
all alone in this house.

Since nine o'clock when I lit the lamp,
the vision of my youthful body
has appeared and found me and reminded me
of closed heavily scented rooms,
and pleasure long past—what audacious pleasure!
And it also brought before my eyes
streets that have now become unrecognizable,
centers full of movement that are ended,
and theaters and cafés that once used to be.

The vision of my youthful body
appeared and brought me also the sad memories;
family mournings, separations,
feelings of my dear ones, feelings
of the dead so little esteemed.

Half past twelve. How the time has passed.
Half past twelve. How the years have passed.

ARISTOBOULUS

The palace is in tears, the king is in tears,
King Herod laments inconsolably,
the entire city is in tears for Aristoboulus
who was so unjustly drowned, by accident,
while playing with his friends in the water.

And when they learn of it in other places too,
when the news is spread up in Syria,
even among the Greeks many will be saddened;
many poets and sculptors will mourn,
for they had heard of the name of Aristoboulus,
and never before had their vision of a young man
compared with such beauty as this boy had;
what statue of a god had Antioch deserved
as fine as this child of Israel?

The First Princess, his mother, the most eminent
Hebrew lady, laments and weeps.
Alexandra laments and weeps over the calamity.—
But when she finds herself alone her sorrow alters.
She groans; she rails; she reviles and utters curses.
How they have deceived her! How they have duped her!
How their purpose has finally been realized!
They have ruined the house of the Asamonaeans.
How the criminal king has achieved his end;
the crafty, the villainous, the wicked.
How he has achieved his end. What an infernal plot
that even Miriam should detect nothing.
Had Miriam detected, had she suspected,
she would have found a way to save her brother;
she is queen after all, she could have done something.
How they will triumph now and secretly gloat,
those wicked women, Cypris and Salome;
those vulgar women, Cypris and Salome.—

And that she should be powerless, and obliged
to pretend that she believes their lies;
not to be able to go before the people,
to go out and shout it to the Hebrews,
to tell, to tell how the murder was done.

AT THE FOOT OF THE HOUSE

Yesterday while walking in an outlying
neighborhood, I passed below the house
I used to frequent when I was very young.
There love with his marvelous strength
had possessed my body.

And yesterday
as I passed by along the old road,
the shops, the sidewalks, the stones,
walls, balconies, and windows
were made beautiful at once by the enchantment of love;
nothing unbeautiful remained there.

And as I stood there, and looked at the door,
and stood, and lingered below the house,
all of my being gave back
the delightful stored-up sensual emotion.

AEMILIANUS MONAÊ ALEXANDRIAN, A.D. 628–655

With words, with my face, and my ways
I shall make me an excellent panoply;
in this way, I shall face evil men
without any fear or weakness.

They will want to harm me. But of all
who approach me none will know
where my wounds are, my vulnerable parts,
beneath the lies that will cover me.—

Boastful words of Aemilianus Monaê.
I wonder did he ever make this panoply?
At all events, he did not wear it much.
He died in Sicily, when he was twenty-seven.

OF THE HEBREWS (A.D. 50)

Painter and poet, runner and discus thrower,
Janthis, son of Antony, handsome as Endymion.
From a family friendly to the synagogue.

"My proudest days are those
when I leave off the aesthetic quest,
when I abandon the beautiful, hard hellenism,
with its sovereign absorption
in perfectly wrought and perishable white limbs.
And I become the one I would always
want to remain: of the Hebrews,
of the holy Hebrews, the son."

His declaration was most ardent. "Always
to remain of the Hebrews, of the holy Hebrews.—"

But he did not stay such a man at all.
The Hedonism and the Arts of Alexandria
kept him their devoted child.

TO REMAIN

It must have been one o'clock in the morning,
or half past one.

In a corner of the tavern;
behind the wooden partition.
Aside from the two of us the shop was completely deserted.
A kerosene lamp scarcely lighted it.
Dozing, at the doorway, the waiter dead for sleep.

No one would have seen us. But already
we had excited ourselves so much,
that we became unfit for precautions.

Our clothes were half opened—they were not many
for a divine month of July was scorching hot.

Enjoyment of the flesh between
our half-opened clothes;
quick baring of the flesh—the vision of what
occurred twenty-six years ago; and has now come
to remain among these verses.

IMENUS

". . . Sensual delight sickly and corruptively acquired
should be loved even more;
rarely finding the body that feels as it would wish—
sickly and corruptive, it furnishes
an erotic intensity, unknown to health . . ."

Extract from a letter
of young Imenus (of a patrician family) notorious
in Syracuse for his wantonness,
in the wanton times of Michael the Third.

ON THE SHIP

Certainly this little drawing
in pencil resembles him.

Hurriedly drawn, on the deck of the ship
one enchanting afternoon.
The Ionian Sea all around us.

It resembles him. But I recall him as handsomer.
He was sensitive to the point of suffering,
and that illumined his expression.
He comes to mind as handsomer
now that my soul evokes him out of Time.

Out of Time. All of these things are exceedingly old—
the sketch, and the ship, and the afternoon.

OF DEMETRIUS SOTER, 162–150 B.C.

His every expectation came out wrong!

He used to dream he would do famous works,
end the humiliation that oppresses his land
ever since the battle of Magnesia.
See that Syria would be a mighty nation again,
with her armies, with her fleets,
with her great fortresses, with her wealth.

He suffered, he felt much bitterness in Rome
as he sensed in the talk of his friends,
young people of prominent houses,
amid all the delicacy and politeness
that they kept showing to him, the son
of the King Seleucus Philopator—
as he sensed however that there was always
a covert indifference to the hellenized dynasties;
that had declined, that are not for serious works,
for the leadership of peoples, quite unfit.
He would withdraw alone, and grow indignant, and he swore
that things would not be at all as they thought;
look, he has determination;
he will struggle, perform, exalt.

If only he could find a way to get to the East,
to succeed in escaping from Italy—
and all the vitality he has
in his soul, all this energy
he will communicate to the people.

Ah, if only he could find himself in Syria!
He was so young when he left his country,
that he can barely remember its face.
But in his thought he always studied it
as something sacred you approach with adoration,

as a vision of a lovely land, as a spectacle
of Greek cities and harbors.—

And now?
Now despair and grief.
The young men in Rome were right.
It is not possible for dynasties to survive
that the Macedonian Conquest gave rise to.

No matter: He himself had tried,
he had struggled as much as he could.
And in his dark discouragement,
one thing alone he reckons
with pride, that, even in his failure,
to the world he shows the same indomitable manliness.

The rest—were dreams and vain efforts.
This Syria—scarcely looks like his own country,
it is the land of Heracleides and Balas.

AFTERNOON SUN

This room, how well I know it.
Now this one and the one next door are rented
as business offices. The whole house has become
offices for agents, and merchants, and Companies.

Ah, this room, how familiar it is.

Near the door over here was a sofa,
and in front of it a Turkish rug;
close by, the shelf with two yellow vases.
On the right; no, opposite, a closet with a mirror.
In the center the table where he used to write;
and the three large wicker chairs.
Beside the window was the bed
where we made love so many times.

The poor objects must still be somewhere around.

Beside the window was the bed;
the afternoon sun reached it down to the middle.

. . . One afternoon at four o'clock we separated
for a week only . . . Ah me,
that week lasted forever.

IF DEAD INDEED

"Where has he retired, where did the Sage vanish?
After his numerous miracles,
the fame of his teaching
that spread over so many nations,
he suddenly hid and no one has learned
with certainty what became of him
(nor has anyone ever seen his grave).
Some spread the rumor that he died at Ephesus.
But Damis did not record it; Damis wrote
nothing on the death of Apollonius.
Others said he vanished at Lindus.
Or perhaps that other story
is true, that he was risen in Crete,
at the ancient shrine of Dictynna.—
But still we have his miraculous,
his supernatural apparition
to a young student at Tyana.—
Perhaps the time has not come for him to return
that he may be seen once more in the world;
or transfigured, perhaps, he goes about
among us incognito.—But he will reappear,
as he used to be, teaching the right; and then of course
he will restore the worship of our gods,
and our elegant Grecian ceremonies."

So he mused in his penurious dwelling—
after a reading of Philostratus
"On Apollonius of Tyana"—
One of the few pagans,
the very few pagans who still remained. Besides—an insignificant
man and cowardly—outwardly
he too acted the Christian and attended church.
It was the period when the aged Justin
reigned in extreme piety,
and when Alexandria, a god-fearing city,
abhorred all wretched idolators.

ANNA COMNENA

Anna Comnena in her *Alexiad's* prologue,
laments her widowhood.

Her soul is in a dizzy state. "And I
wet my eyes," she tells us, "with rivulets
of tears. . . . Alas for the waves" in her life,
"Alas for the revolutions." Pain burns her
"to her bones and her marrow and the cleaving of her soul."

More like the truth, however, is that this ambitious woman
knew only one mortal sorrow;
she had only one deep longing
(though she never admits it), this haughty Greek woman,
that she was never able, with all her dexterity,
to acquire the Kingship; it was snatched
almost out of her hands by the impertinent John.

FOR THEM TO COME

One candle is enough. Its dim light
is more appropriate, it will be kindlier
when Shadows come, the Shadows of Love.

One candle is enough. Tonight the room
must not have too much light. Immersed entirely in revery
and in suggestion, and in the low light—
Thus deep in revery I will dream a vision so

that Shadows may come, the Shadows of love.

YOUNG MEN OF SIDON (A.D. 400)

The actor they had brought to entertain them
also recited several choice epigrams.

The drawing room opened out on the garden;
and it had a light fragrance of flowers
that mingled with the fragrance
of the five perfumed young Sidonians.

They read Meleager, and Crinagoras, and Rhianos.
But when the actor had recited,
"Here lies the Athenian Aeschylus son of Euphorion"—
(stressing perhaps more than necessary
the words "famous for his valor," the "sacred Marathonian grove"),
a spirited young man, a fanatic of letters,
leaped up at once and shouted,

"Oh, that quatrain does not please me.
Somehow such phrases seem to betray cowardice.
Give—I say—all your strength to your work,
all your care, and again—remember your work
in your time of trial, or when your hour is near.
This is what I expect and demand of you.
And not to dismiss entirely from your mind
the brilliant Word of Tragedy—
that Agamemnon, that remarkable Prometheus,
those presentations of Orestes, Cassandra,
The Seven Against Thebes—and as a reminder,
only note that in the ranks of soldiers,
among the masses, you too fought Datis and Artaphernes."

DARIUS

The poet Phernazis is composing
the important part of his epic poem.
How Darius, the son of Hystaspes,
assumed the kingdom of the Persians.
(Our glorious king Mithridates, hailed as
Dionysus and Eupator, is descended from him.)
But here we have need of philosophy; we must analyze
the sentiments that Darius must have felt:
perhaps arrogance and drunkenness; but no—rather
like understanding of the vanity of grandeurs.
The poet reflects profoundly on the matter.

But he is interrupted by his servant who enters
running, and announces the gravest news.
The war with the Romans has begun.
The bulk of our army has crossed the frontiers.

The poet is dumbfounded. What a catastrophe!
How can our glorious king Mithridates,
hailed as Dionysus and Eupator,
possibly occupy himself now with Greek poems?
In the midst of a war—just imagine, Greek poems.

Phernazis is impatient. How unfortunate!
At a time when he was positive that with his "Darius"
he would distinguish himself, and shut forever
the mouths of his critics, the envious ones.
What a delay, what a delay to his plans.

But if it were only a delay, it would still be all right.
But let us see if we have any security at all
in Amisus. It is not a very well-fortified city.
The Romans are the most horrible enemies.
Can we get the best of them, we

Cappadocians? Is that ever possible?
Can we measure ourselves in a time like this against legions?
Mighty Gods, protectors of Asia, help us.—

Yet amid all his agitation and the trouble,
the poetic idea persistently comes and goes.—
The most probable, surely, is arrogance and drunkenness;
Darius must have felt arrogance and drunkenness.

A BYZANTINE NOBLE IN EXILE WRITING VERSES

Let the flippant call me flippant.
In serious matters I have always been
most diligent. And I will insist that
no one is more familiar than I
with Fathers or Scriptures, or the Synodical Canons.
In each of his doubts,
in each difficulty concerning church matters,
Botaneiatis consulted me, me first of all.
But exiled here (may the malevolent Irene Doukaina
suffer for it), and dreadfully bored,
it is not at all peculiar that I amuse myself
composing sestets and octets—
that I amuse myself with mythological tales
of Hermes, Apollo, and Dionysus,
or the heroes of Thessaly and the Peloponnese;
and that I compose impeccable iambics,
such as—permit me to say—Constantinople's men of letters cannot compose.
This very accuracy, probably, is the cause of their censure.

FAVOR OF ALEXANDER BALAS

O, I am not upset that a wheel of my chariot
is broken, and I have lost a foolish victory.
I will spend the night with fine wines
and amid lovely roses. Antioch belongs to me.
I am the young man most glorified.
I am Balas's weakness, his adored one.
Tomorrow, you'll see, they'll say that the contest was unfair.
(But if I were coarse, and had ordered it in secret—
the flatterers would have voted first prize even to my crippled
chariot.)

I BROUGHT TO ART

I sit and meditate. I brought to art
desires and feelings— some things half seen,
faces or lines; some indistinct memories
of unfulfilled loves. Let me rely on her.
She knows how to fashion a Figure of Beauty;
almost imperceptibly rounding out life,
combining impressions, combining the days.

THEIR BEGINNING

The fulfillment of their deviate, sensual delight
is done. They rose from the mattress,
and they dress hurriedly without speaking.
They leave the house separately, furtively; and as
they walk somewhat uneasily on the street, it seems
as if they suspect that something about them betrays
into what kind of bed they fell a little while back.

But how the life of the artist has gained.
Tomorrow, the next day, years later, the vigorous verses
will be composed that had their beginning here.

DEMARATUS

The subject, The Character of Demaratus,
that Porphyry suggested in a conversation,
thus the young sophist stated it
(intending later to develop it rhetorically).

"First in the court of King Darius, and then
a courtier to King Xerxes
and now with Xerxes and his army,
see at long last Demaratus will be vindicated.

"A great injustice was done to him.
He was the son of Ariston. Shamelessly
his enemies had bribed the oracle.
And they were not content to have deprived him of the kingship,
but when he had finally submitted, and decided
to live with resignation as a private citizen,
they had to insult him too before the people,
they had to humble him publicly at the feast.

"Therefore he serves Xerxes with great zeal.
He too will return to Sparta,
with the mighty Persian army;
and become a king as before, how he will
turn him out at once, how he will humiliate
that intriguer Leotychides."

And his days pass fraught with anxiety;
counseling the Persians, explaining to them
how they should act to conquer Greece.

"Many cares, much thought, and this is why
the days of Demaratus are full of boredom;
many cares, much thought, and this is why
Demaratus has not one moment of joy;

for what he feels is not joy
(it is not; he will not admit it;
how can he call it joy? His misfortune has reached its peak)
when events plainly prove to him
that the Greeks will be victorious."

AN ARTISAN OF WINE-MIXING BOWLS

On this lovely wine-mixing bowl   of the purest silver—
that was made for the house   of Heraclides,
where excellent taste   prevails above all—
you see elegant flowers,   and brooks, and thyme,
and in the center I have placed   a handsome young man,
naked and amorous;   one of his legs is still
plunged in the water.—   I have prayed, O Memory,
to find in you the best guide,   that I might make the face
of the young man that I loved   as it once used to be.
The difficulty was great   because almost
fifteen years   have passed since the day
when he fell, a soldier,   in the defeat of Magnesia.

MELANCHOLY OF JASON, SON OF CLEANDER; POET IN COMMAGENE; A.D. 595

The growing old of my body and my face
is a wound from a hideous knife.
I no longer have any endurance.
I take refuge in you, Art of Poetry,
who know a little something about drugs,
and attempts to numb suffering, in Imagination and Word.

It is a wound from a hideous knife.—
Fetch your drugs, Art of Poetry,
that make one unaware—for a while—of the wound.—

FROM THE SCHOOL OF THE RENOWNED PHILOSOPHER

He remained a student of Ammonius Saccas for two years;
but he became bored with philosophy and with Saccas.

Then he entered politics.
But he abandoned that. The Eparch was an idiot;
and those around him solemn-faced official blockheads;
their Greek was thrice barbarous, the sorry wretches.

The Church attracted his curiosity
a little; to have himself baptized
and pass as a Christian. But soon he
changed his mind. He would surely have a falling out
with his parents, ostentatiously pagan;
and they would stop—a horrible thing—
their very generous allowances to him at once.

But nevertheless he had to do something. He became a customer
of the corrupt houses of Alexandria,
of every secret den of debauchery.

Destiny had been kind to him in this regard;
she had endowed him with a rarely handsome face.
And he delighted in the divine gift.

At the very least his beauty would endure
for another ten years. And after that—
perhaps he would return once more to Saccas.

And if in the meantime the old man should die,
he would go to another philosopher or sophist;
the appropriate person is always found.

Or in the end, it is even likely he might
return to politics—laudably remembering
the traditions of his family,
his duty to country, and other similar high-sounding matters.

TO ANTIOCHUS EPIPHANES

The young man of Antioch said to the King,
"A beloved hope pulses in the depths of my heart;
once more the Macedonians, Antiochus Epiphanes,
the Macedonians are involved in the major struggle.
If only they would triumph— I would willingly give
anyone the lion and the horses, the Pan of coral,
and the elegant palace, and the Tyrian gardens,
and all else you have given me, Antiochus Epiphanes."

Perhaps for a brief moment the King was a little moved.
But at once he remembered his father and brother,
and he did not even reply. An eavesdropper might go
and repeat something.— Besides, as was natural,
the horrible ending came quite suddenly at Pydna.

THOSE WHO FOUGHT FOR THE ACHAEAN LEAGUE

Valiant are you who fought and fell in glory;
fearless of those who were everywhere victorious.
If Daos and Critolaos were at fault, you are blameless.
When the Greeks want to boast,
"Our nation turns out such men as these," they will say
of you. So marvelous will be your praise—

Written in Alexandria by an Achaean;
in the seventh year of Ptolemy Lathyrus.

IN AN OLD BOOK

In an old book—about a hundred years old—
forgotten among its pages,
I found a water color without signature.
It must have been the work of a very able artist.
It had as its title, "A Presentation of Love."

But more fitting would have been, "Of Utter Sensual Love."

For it was evident when you looked at the work
(the artist's idea was easily understood)
that the young man in the painting was not destined
to be one of those who loves more or less healthily,
remaining within the limits of the more or less
permissible—with chestnut, deep-colored eyes;
with the exquisite beauty of his face,
the beauty of deviate attractions;
with his ideal lips that offer
sensual delight to a beloved body;
with his ideal limbs created for beds which
current morality brands as shameless.

EPITAPH OF ANTIOCHUS, KING OF COMMAGENE

When she returned, disconsolate, from his funeral,
the sister of the man who in life had been mild and meek,
the most scholarly Antiochus, King of Commagene,
wanted an epitaph for him. And the Ephesian
sophist Callistratus—who often sojourned
in the little state of Commagene, and had been shown
hospitality gladly and repeatedly in the royal house—
wrote it, according to the suggestions of the Syrian courtiers,
and sent it to the venerable old lady.

"Let the glory of Antiochus the benevolent King
be praised worthily, O Commagenians.
He was the provident governor of our country.
He was just, wise, courageous.
And he was moreover that best of all, a Greek—
humanity has no more honorable quality;
those beyond are found among the gods."

JULIAN SEEING INDIFFERENCE

"Considering then that there is much indifference
on our part toward the gods"—he speaks with grave mien.
Indifference. Well, but then what did he expect?
He could organize religion to his heart's content,
he could write to the High Priest of Galatia to his heart's content,
or to others such as these, exhorting and guiding.
His friends were not Christians;
that was positive. But they were not able as he was
(nurtured in Christianity) to give a performance
in a system of a new church,
as ridiculous in conception as in application.
They were Greeks after all. Nothing in excess, Augustus.

THEATER OF SIDON (A.D. 400)

Son of an esteemed citizen— above all, a handsome
young man of the theater, agreeable in many a way,
once in a while I compose in the Greek language
very daring verses, which I circulate
clandestinely, to be sure— Gods! Those dark-clad people
chattering about morals— mustn't catch sight of these
verses about pleasure choice pleasure
leading to sterile love and love that is rejected.

IN DESPAIR

He has lost him completely.   And now he is seeking
on the lips of   every new lover
the lips of his beloved;   in the embrace
of every new lover   he seeks to be deluded
that he is the same lad,   that it is to him he is yielding.

He has lost him completely,   as if he had never been at all.
For he wanted—so he said—   he wanted to be saved
from the stigmatized,   the sick sensual delight;
from the stigmatized,   sensual delight of shame.
There was still time—   as he said—to be saved.

He has lost him completely,   as if he had never been at all.
In his imagination,   in his delusions,
on the lips of others   it is his lips he is seeking;
he is longing to feel again   the love he has known.

JULIAN IN NICOMEDEIA

Aimless and perilous things.
The praises for the ideals of the Greeks.

The miracles and visits to the temples
of the pagans. The enthusiasms for the gods of antiquity.

The frequent conversations with Chrisanthius.
The theories of Maximus—the philosopher—clever besides.

And here is the result. Gallus manifests great
uneasiness. Constantius has some suspicion.

Ah, his counselors were not at all wise.
This history—says Mardonius—has gone too far,

and its uproar must cease at all costs.—
Julian returns once more as a reader

to the church of Nicomedeia,
where in a loud voice and with deep reverence

he reads the Holy Scriptures,
and the people admire his Christian piety.

BEFORE TIME CHANGES THEM

They were both deeply grieved   at their separation.
They did not desire it;   it was circumstances.
The needs of a living   obliged one of them
to go to a distant place—   New York or Canada.
Their love certainly   was not what it had been before;
for the attraction   had gradually waned,
for love's attraction   had considerably waned.
But they did not desire   to be separated.
It was circumstances.—   Or perhaps Destiny
had appeared as an artist   separating them now
before their feeling should fade,   before Time had changed them;
so each for the other will   remain forever as he had been,
a handsome young man   of twenty-four years.

IN ALEXANDRIA, 31 B.C.

From his tiny village, close to the suburbs,
and still covered with dust from the journey

the trader arrives. And "Frankincense!" and "Gum!"
"The Finest Olive Oil!" "Scent for the Hair!"

He cries on the streets. But the great clamor of the mob,
the medley of music and the parades, would they let him be heard?

The crowd jostles him, pulls him along, knocks against him.
And then when he is perfectly befuddled, "What is this madness?" he
asks.
One of them hurls at him also the gigantic lie
of the palace—that in Greece Antony is victorious.

JOHN CANTACUZENUS TRIUMPHS

He sees the fields that he can still call his own
with the wheat, with the cattle, with the fruit-laden
trees. And a little beyond, his paternal home,
full of clothes and costly furniture, and silverware.

They will take them from him—Jesus Christ!—they will take them
from him now.

Would Cantacuzenus feel pity for him perhaps
if he went and fell at his feet? They say he is lenient,
very lenient. But those around him? But the army?—
Or, should he prostrate himself and plead before Kyria Irene?

Idiot! To have become involved in Anna's party—
if only Kyr Andronicus had not lived
to marry her. Have we seen any good come out
of her behavior, have we seen any humanity?
Why even the Franks no longer esteem her.
Her plans are preposterous, her whole preparation is absurd.
While they threatened the world from Constantinople.
Cantacuzenus annihilated them, Kyr John annihilated them.

And to think he had meant to go over to Kyr John's
side! He would have done it too. And he would have been happy
now,
a great nobleman all this while, and solidly established,
if at the very last moment the bishop had not succeeded
in persuading him with his priestly impressiveness,
with his misinformations from beginning to end,
and with his promises, and his imbecilities.

HE CAME TO READ

He came to read. Two or three volumes
are open; historians and poets.
But he had barely read for ten minutes,
when he laid them aside. He is dozing
on the sofa. He is entirely devoted to books—
but he is twenty-three years old, and he is very handsome;
and this afternoon love passed
through his ideal flesh, his lips.
Through his flesh that is sheer beauty,
the fever of love passed; without
his feeling derisive shame for the form of his enjoyment . . .

BY AN ITALIAN SHORE

Cemos, son of Menedorus,   a young Italian of
Greek blood, passes his life   immersed in amusements;
as these young men   from Greater Greece,
raised in great wealth   are accustomed to do.

But today he is especially,   despite his natural self,
preoccupied and dejected.   All along the seashore,
in sheer melancholy   he watches them unload
vessels with booty taken   from the Peloponnese.

Spoils from Greece;   the booty from Corinth.

Ah, surely on this day   it is not permissible,
it is not possible   for this Italian of
Greek blood to have any   desire for amusements.

OF COLORED GLASS

One detail stirs me to the extreme
in the coronation, at Blachernae, of John Cantacuzenus
and Irene, daughter of Andronicus Assan.
Since they had only a few precious stones
(great was the poverty of our unfortunate state)
they wore artificial gems. A mass of bits of glass,
pieces of red, green, or blue. As I see it,
these tiny pieces of colored glass
have nothing in them that is humiliating
or unseemly. On the contrary they look
like a sorrowful protest
against the unjust wretchedness of those who are crowned.
They are the symbols of what it is fitting for them to have,
of what it was certainly proper for them to have
at the coronation of a Kyr John Cantacuzenus,
a Kyria Irene, daughter of Andronicus Assan.

TEMETHOS OF ANTIOCH, A.D. 400

Verses of young Temethos   the lovelorn poet.
With the title "Emonides"—   the beloved companion
of Antiochus Epiphanes;   a very good-looking
young man from Samosata.   But if these verses have
turned out ardent and moving   it is because Emonides
(from that ancient epoch   in one hundred thirty-seven
of the kingship of the Greeks!—   perhaps a bit earlier)
was added to the poem   merely as a name;
yet a proper-enough name.   The poem expresses
a certain love of Temethos.   A beautiful love
and worthy of him.   We, the initiate,
his intimate friends;   we, the initiate,
we know well for whom   the verses were written.
The naïve Antiocheans   read only "Emonides."

APOLLONIUS OF TYANA IN RHODES

Apollonius was talking about proper
education and conduct with a young man
who was constructing a luxurious house
in Rhodes. "As for me," the Tyanian said in the end,
"when I enter a temple, however little it
may be, I would much rather look at
a statue made of ivory and gold,
than see, in a large temple, a vulgar statue of clay."

The "clay" and the "vulgar," the detestable,
that already knavishly deceive a good many
(without enough training). The "clay" and the "vulgar."

IN THE MONOTONOUS VILLAGE

In the monotonous village where he works—
an employee in a general store;
so very young—where he still has to wait
for another two or three months to pass,
another two or three months for business to slacken a bit,
so that he may dash to town and fling himself
at once into activity and amusement;
in the monotonous village where he waits—
lovelorn he fell on his bed tonight,
all his youth ablaze with desire of the flesh,
all his beautiful youth in a beautiful intensity.
And in his sleep, voluptuousness came to him;
in his sleep he sees and possesses the figure and flesh he craved. . . .

THE 25TH YEAR OF HIS LIFE

He goes regularly to the tavern
where they had met each other the month before.
He inquired; but they had nothing precise to tell him.
From their words, he understood that his friend had made the acquaintance
of some entirely unknown person,
one of the many unknown and suspicious
youthful figures that used to go by there.
But he goes to the tavern regularly, at night,
and he sits and looks toward the entrance;
he looks toward the entrance to the point of weariness.
He may walk in. He may still come tonight.

For almost three weeks he does this.
His mind has grown sick from lust.
The kisses have stayed on his mouth.
All his flesh suffers from the persistent desire.
The touch of that body is over him.
He longs for union with him again.

Naturally he tries not to betray himself.
But sometimes he is almost indifferent.
Besides, he knows to what he is exposing himself,
he has made up his mind. It is not unlikely that this life
of his may bring him to a disastrous scandal.

KLEITOS' ILLNESS

Kleitos, a sympathetic young man,
about twenty-three years of age—
with an excellent upbringing, with rare Greek learning—
is critically ill. The fever that decimated
Alexandria this year found him.

Fever found him morally exhausted also,
sick with grief that his companion, a young actor,
had ceased to love him and to desire him.

He is critically ill, and his parents tremble.

And an aged servant who had raised him
also trembles for the life of Kleitos.
In her terrible anxiety
there comes to her mind an idol
she worshipped as a child, before coming here, as a servant,
in this house of illustrious Christians, and turning Christian.
Secretly she takes some pancakes, some wine and honey.
She brings them before the idol. She chants all the prayerful
tunes she remembers, beginnings, ends, or middles. The idiot
does not understand that the black demon cares little
whether a Christian is cured or is not cured.

IN THE TAVERNS

I wallow in the taverns   and in the brothels
of Beirut.   I did not want to remain
in Alexandria.   Tamides deserted me;
and he went off with the son   of the Eparch to acquire
a villa on the Nile,   a mansion in the city.
It wouldn't be right for me   to remain in Alexandria.—
I wallow in the taverns   and in the brothels
of Beirut.   I live abjectly
in shabby debauchery.   The only thing that saves me,
like a constant beauty,   like a fragrance that has
remained on my flesh,   is that I possessed Tamides
for two full years,   the most marvelous young man,
mine not merely for a house,   or a villa on the Nile.

SOPHIST LEAVING SYRIA

Distinguished sophist   who are now leaving Syria,
with the intention to write   a work about our Antioch,
it will be worth mentioning   Mebes in your work.
The illustrious Mebes   who is undeniably
the handsomest young man,   and the most beloved,
in the whole of Antioch.   To none of the other youth
leading the same life,   do they pay as high a price
as they pay him.   To possess Mebes
for only two or three days   very often they give him
as much as a hundred staters.—   I said, in Antioch;
but in Alexandria too,   but even in Rome also,
no young man will be found   as desirable as Mebes.

IN A TOWNSHIP OF ASIA MINOR

The news of the outcome of the naval battle, at Actium,
was most certainly unexpected.
But there is no need to compose a new address.
Only the name needs to be changed. There, in the last
lines, instead of "Having liberated the Romans
from the ruinous Octavius,
that parody, as it were, of Caesar,"
now we will put, "Having liberated the Romans
from the ruinous Antony."
The whole text fits in beautifully.

"To the conqueror, the most glorious,
unexcelled in every military enterprise,
admirable in political exploits,
in whose behalf the deme fervently wished
for his triumph over Antony,"
here, as we have stated, is the change: "To Caesar
regarded as the perfect gift of Jupiter—
the powerful protector of the Greeks,
to him who renders honor to our Greek customs;
beloved in every Greek land,
eminently cited for prideful eulogy,
and for the extensive recounting of his deeds
in the Greek language in verse and in prose;
in the *Greek language*, the messenger of fame,"
et cetera, et cetera. Everything fits in fine.

JULIAN AND THE PEOPLE OF ANTIOCH

The CHI, they say, had never harmed their city, nor the KAPPA. And we, finding the explanation by chance, were taught that these were initial letters of two names; one stood for Christ, the other for Constantinius.
JULIAN'S *Misopôgôn*

Was it ever possible that they should renounce
their lovely way of life; the variety of their
daily amusement; their magnificent theater
where a union of the Arts was taking place
with the amorous tendencies of the flesh!

They were immoral to a point—and possibly to a great
degree. But they had the satisfaction of knowing
that their life was the *much talked about* life of Antioch,
rich in pleasures, perfectly elegant in every way.

To renounce all these, to turn to what after all?

To his airy chatter about false gods;
to his tiresome self-centered chatter;
to his childish fear of the theater;
his graceless prudery; his ridiculous beard?

Ah most certainly they preferred the CHI,
ah most certainly they preferred the KAPPA; a hundred times.

A GREAT PROCESSION OF PRIESTS AND LAYMEN

A procession of priests and laymen,
all the professions represented,
goes through the streets, the squares, and portals
of the celebrated city of Antioch.
At the head of the impressive, great procession,
a handsome young man, dressed all in white, carries
in hands uplifted the Cross,
the power and our hope, the Holy Cross.
The pagans who were formerly so arrogant,
now diffident and timid, hastily
draw away from the procession.
Far from us, let them always remain far from us
(as long as they do not renounce their error).
The Holy Cross advances. In every neighborhood
of the city where Christians live in piety
it carries consolation and joy.
They come out, the pious ones, to the doors of their houses
and full of exultation they worship it—
the power, and the salvation of the universe, the Cross.—

It is an annual Christian festival.
But today, see, it is celebrated more brilliantly.
The state has finally been delivered.
The most wicked, the detestable
Julian reigns no more.

Let us pray for the most pious Jovian.

PRIEST AT THE SERAPEUM

The good old man my father
who loved me the same always;
I weep for the good old man my father
who died the day before yesterday, just before dawn.

O Jesus Christ, my daily effort
is to observe the precepts
of Thy most holy church in every act of mine,
in every word, in every single thought.
And all those who renounce Thee,
I shun them.—But now I bewail;
I lament, O Christ, for my father
even though he was—a horrible thing to say—
a priest at the accursed Serapeum.

ANNA DALASSENE

In the royal edict which Alexius Comnenus issued
to render brilliant homage to his mother,
the very sagacious Lady Anna Dalassené—
distinguished in her deeds, in her ways—
there are various laudatory phrases:
here let us convey of them
one beautiful and noble phrase:
"Those cold words 'mine' or 'yours' were never spoken."

GREEK SINCE ANCIENT TIMES

Antioch is boastful   of its magnificent buildings,
and of its beautiful streets;   of the marvelous countryside
surrounding it,   and the great multitude
of its inhabitants.   It boasts that it is the seat
of illustrious kings;   and of its artists
and the wise men it has,   and of its immensely rich
and circumspect merchants.   However, most incomparable
of all, Antioch boasts   that it has been a Greek
city since ancient times;   related to Argus:
of that Ione which   was founded by the Argive
colonists in honor   of the daughter of Inachus.

DAYS OF 1901

This he had in him that set him apart,
that in spite of all his dissoluteness
and his great experience in love,
despite the habitual harmony
that existed between his attitude and his age
there happened to be moments—however,
rarest moments, to be sure—when he gave the
impression of a flesh almost untouched.

The beauty of his twenty-nine years,
so tested by sensual delight,
at moments paradoxically recalled
a young man who—rather gawkily—surrenders
his pure body to love for the very first time.

TWO YOUNG MEN 23 TO 24

He had been in the café since ten-thirty,
expecting to see him come in presently.
Midnight went—and he still waited for him.
Half past one went; the café was
almost entirely empty.
He grew weary of reading newspapers
mechanically. Of his three solitary shillings,
only one was left him: he had waited so long,
he had spent the others on coffees and cognac.
He had smoked all his cigarettes.
Such waiting was exhausting him. For
as he was also alone for hours
troublesome thoughts took hold of him
of the life that had led him astray.

But when he saw his friend enter—instantly
fatigue, boredom, thoughts vanished.

His friend brought him unexpected news.
He had won sixty pounds at the gambling-house.

Their handsome faces, their marvelous youth,
the sensitive love each felt for the other
were refreshed, reanimated, fortified
by the sixty pounds of the gambling-house.

And full of joy and vigor, feeling, and beauty
they went—not to the homes of their honorable families
(where besides, they were no longer wanted):
but to a friend's house, a very particular
house of depravity, and they asked for
a bedroom, and expensive drinks, and again they drank.

And when the expensive drinks were finished,
and since it was almost four o'clock in the morning,
they gave themselves happily to love.

DAYS OF 1896

He was utterly humiliated.   An erotic bent of his,
one sternly forbidden   and most scorned
(but innate nevertheless)   there was a reason for it:
the community was   very puritanical.
Little by little he lost   the bit of money he had;
then he lost his position,   and then his reputation.
He was getting close to thirty   without ever having finished
a year at one job,   at least that anyone knew of.
On occasion he earned   his expenses from
interventions that   are considered shameful.
He became such a character   that were you seen with him
often, you would probably be   seriously compromised.

But this is not all of it;   that would not be quite fair.
Even more appropriate   is the mention of his beauty.
There is another aspect   that puts him in a better light
and makes him seem sympathetic;   makes him seem to be a very simple,
genuine child of love   who unquestionably placed
higher than his honor,   and his reputation too,
the pure sensual delight   of his pure flesh.

Above his reputation?   But the community that was
so puritanical   made stupid comparisons.

A YOUNG MAN SKILLED IN THE ART OF THE WORD

Henceforth brain, toil as well as you can.—
A half-enjoyment is wasting him.
He is in a nervous state.
Every day he kisses the beloved face,
his hands are placed on the impeccable limbs.
He has never loved with such a great degree of
passion. But the beautiful consummation of love
is lacking; the consummation is lacking
that must be intensely desired by both of them.

(They are not both equally given to deviate sensual pleasure.
Him alone it has utterly mastered.)

So he is wasted, and he is completely unnerved.
Besides he is out of work; and that has much to do with it.
With difficulty he borrows some small
sums of money (sometimes he practically
begs for it) and pseudo-supports himself.
He kisses the adored lips; on that exquisite
body—that now however he senses
is only consenting—he takes his pleasure.
And then he drinks and he smokes; he drinks and he smokes;
and he drags himself through the cafés all day long,
he drags with boredom the languor of his beauty.—
Henceforth brain, toil as well as you can.

IN A FAMOUS GREEK COLONY, 200 B.C.

There is not the slightest doubt
that things in the Colony are not going as desired,
though in some way or other we are going forward;
perhaps, as many people think, the time has come
to call in a Political Reformer.

However, the handicap and the hardship
are that these Reformers make
a big story out of everything.
(It would be a blessing if one never
needed them.) For everything,
for the least thing, they inquire and investigate,
and immediately they think of radical reforms,
with the request that they be executed without delay.

They also have a bent for sacrifices.
GIVE UP THAT POSSESSION OF YOURS;
YOUR PROPERTY IS UNSAFE:
IT IS PRECISELY SUCH HOLDINGS THAT HARM THE COLONIES.
GIVE UP THIS REVENUE
AND THIS OTHER THAT GOES WITH IT
AND THIS THIRD THAT FOLLOWS: AS A NATURAL RESULT;
TRUE, THEY ARE SUBSTANTIAL, BUT WHAT CAN ONE DO?
THEY CREATE A HEAVY RESPONSIBILITY FOR YOU.

And as they proceed with their investigation,
they find and refind excesses that they seek to stop,
things however that are hard for one to suppress.

And when, at long last, they finish their work,
and after having defined and minutely trimmed everything,
they go, also carrying off their rightful salary,
now let us see what still remains, after
such surgical ingenuity.—

Perhaps the time has not arrived as yet.
We must not rush ourselves; haste is a perilous thing.
Premature measures bring repentance.
To be sure and unfortunately, the Colony has many shortcomings.
However, is there anything human without imperfection?
And, after all, look, we are going forward.

PICTURE OF A 23-YEAR-OLD YOUTH PAINTED BY HIS FRIEND OF THE SAME AGE, AN AMATEUR

He finished the painting   yesterday noon. Now
he studies it in detail.   He has painted him in a
gray unbuttoned coat,   a deep gray; without
any vest or any tie.   With a rose-colored shirt;
open at the collar,   so something might be seen
also of the beauty   of his chest, of his neck.
The right temple   is almost entirely
covered by his hair,   his beautiful hair
(parted in the manner   he prefers it this year).
There is the completely   voluptuous tone
he wanted to put into it   when he was doing the eyes,
when he was doing the lips. . . .   His mouth, the lips
that are made for consummation,   for choice love-making.

UNDERSTOOD NOT

Concerning our religious beliefs—
the empty-headed Julian said: "I read, I understood,
I condemned." As if the most ludicrous man
had annihilated us, with his "I condemned."

However such clevernesses carry no weight with us
Christians. "You read, but understood not; for if you had understood,
you would not have condemned," we retorted at once.

CIMON, SON OF LEARCHUS, A 22-YEAR-OLD STUDENT OF GREEK LETTERS (IN CYRENE)

"The end of my life came when I was happy.
Hermeteles had me as his inseparable friend.
During my very last days, in spite of always feigning
that he was not uneasy, I often noticed
his eyes red from weeping. When he thought that I had been
asleep for a short while, he would fall like one insane
at the edge of my bed. But the two of us were
young men of the same age, twenty-three years old.
Destiny is a traitor. Perhaps some other passion
might have taken Hermeteles from me.
I really ended well; in undivided love."—

I, his grief-stricken cousin, his cousin Cimon,
have received this epitaph for Marylos Aristodemus
who died a month ago in Alexandria.
The writer, a poet I knew, has sent it to me.
He has sent it to me because he knows that I was
related to Marylos; he didn't know anything else.
My soul is full of sorrow for Marylos.
We grew up together as close as two brothers.
I am deeply grieved. His premature death
has entirely erased in me every resentment . . .
every resentment in me for Marylos—although
he had stolen from me the love of Hermeteles,
and even if Hermeteles should desire me again
it can never be at all the same. I know what a sensitive
character I have. The image of Marylos
will surely come between us, and I will imagine that
he is saying to me, "See now you are satisfied.
See you have taken him again just as you wanted, Cimon.
See henceforth you have no excuse to malign me."

IN SPARTA

King Cleomenes did not know, he did not dare—
he did not know how to put into words such a request
to his own mother: that Ptolemy had demanded
that she be sent to Egypt also and be held a hostage there
as a guarantee of their agreement;
a very humiliating, unseemly matter.
And he was always about to speak; and he always demurred.
And he always started to say it; and he always faltered.

But this superior woman understood him
(besides, she had already heard some rumors about it),
and she encouraged him to explain.
And she laughed; and she said certainly she would go.
And indeed she rejoiced that she was able
still to be useful to Sparta in her old age.

As for the humiliation—well she was indifferent.
Assuredly he, a son of Lagus, born only yesterday,
was unable to understand Spartan pride;
and so his request could not really
humiliate a Great Lady as
illustrious as she; the mother of a Spartan king.

DAYS OF 1909, 1910, 1911

He was the son of a harassed, very destitute
mariner (from an island on the Aegean Sea).
He worked at an ironmonger's. He wore very old clothes.
His work shoes were torn and wretched.
His hands were grimy with rust and oil.

In the evening, when the shop had closed,
if there was something he desired very much,
some rather expensive tie,
some special tie for Sunday,
or if he had seen in a shop window and craved
some beautiful blue shirt,
he would sell his body for a dollar or two.

I ask myself if in the days of antiquity
glorious Alexandria possessed a more superb-looking youth,
a lad more perfect than he—who had been wasted:
Of course, no statue or painting was ever done of him;
cast into the filthy old ironmonger's,
quickly, by heavy labor,
and by common debauchery, so wretched, he was destroyed.

A SOVEREIGN FROM WESTERN LIBYA

Aristomenes, son of Menelaus,
a sovereign from Western Libya,
was generally liked in Alexandria
during the ten days he sojourned there.
Like his name, his dress, also, decorously Greek.
He gladly accepted honors, but
he did not seek them; he was modest.
He would buy Greek books,
especially on history and philosophy.
But above all he was a man of few words.
He must be profound in his thoughts, people said,
and for such men it is natural not to talk much.

He was neither profound in his thoughts, nor anything else.
Just an ordinary, ridiculous man.
He took a Greek name, dressed like the Greeks;
learned more or less to behave like the Greeks;
and his soul shuddered with fear lest he chance
to mar a rather favorable impression
by speaking the Greek language with fearful barbarisms,
and the Alexandrians would find him out,
as is their habit, the horrible wretches.

That is why he restricted himself to a few words,
fearfully observing his cases and pronunciation;
and he suffered not a little having
whole conversations piled up inside him.

ON THE MARCH TO SINOPE

Mithridates, glorious and powerful,
lord of great cities,
possessor of mighty armies and fleets,
on his way to Sinope, happened to pass through
a road in the country, off the beaten path
where a soothsayer had his dwelling.

Mithridates sent one of his officers
to ask the soothsayer how many more good things
he would acquire in the future, how many more powers.

He sent one of his officers, and then
continued his march toward Sinope.

The soothsayer retired to a secret room.
After half an hour or so he came out
in deep thought and said to the officer,
"I could not distinguish with sufficient clarity.
Today is doubtless not an appropriate day.
I saw certain shadowy things. I did not understand well.—
But the king ought to be content, in my opinion, with what he has.
Any more would expose him to great perils.
Officer, remember to tell him this:
In God's name, let him be content with what he has!
Fortune makes unexpected reversals.
Remember to tell King Mithridates this:
Very rarely is found the noble companion of his ancestor
who in the nick of time traces on the earth
with his spear the salutary advice: 'FLEE MITHRIDATES.'"

MYRES: ALEXANDRIA, A.D. 340

When I learned of the misfortune, that Myres was dead,
I paid a visit to his house, though I avoid
going into the homes of the Christians,
especially in time of mournings or feasts.

I stayed in the vestibule. I did not want
to go farther inside, because I had noticed
that the dead boy's relatives kept staring at me
in strange astonishment and displeasure.

They had placed him in a large room,
and from the corner where I stood
I could see a little; expensive carpets everywhere,
and vessels of silver and of gold.

I stood at one end of the vestibule and wept.
And I thought how our reunions and excursions
would no longer be worth while without Myres;
and I thought how I would see him no more
at our fine, immodest all-night revels
enjoying himself, and laughing, and reciting verses
with his perfect sense of Greek rhythm;
and I thought how I had lost his beauty
forever, how I had lost forever
the youth whom I so madly adored.

Some old women near me spoke in low voices
of the last day of his life—
that the name of Christ was constantly on his lips,
that he held a cross in his hands.—
Then into the room entered
four Christian priests fervently saying
prayers and supplications to Jesus,
or to Mary! (I do not know their religion well.)

We knew, of course, that Myres was a Christian.
We knew it from the first moment when he
joined our group, the year before last.
But he lived precisely as we did.
Of all of us, the most addicted to pleasures;
squandering his money recklessly on amusements.
Careless about the world's estimate of him,
he flung himself happily into nocturnal street brawls
every time our gang happened
to meet a hostile gang.
He never spoke of his religion.
Indeed, one time we told him that we
would take him with us to Serapeum.
However, it seemed that our jest
had displeased him: I remember now.
Ah and two other instances now come to mind.
When we offered libations to Poseidon,
he withdrew from our group and turned his eyes elsewhere.
When enthusiastically one of us
said, "May our companions be under
the favor and the protection of the mighty,
the all-beautiful Apollo,"—Myres murmured
(the others did not hear him), "Except for me."

The Christian priests prayed in a loud voice
for the soul of the young man.—
I observed with what care
and with what meticulous attention
for their religious rites they prepared
every detail for the Christian burial.
And suddenly a queer impression
seized me. I had the vague feeling
that Myres was leaving my side;
I felt that he was united, a Christian,
with his own people, and I was becoming
a *stranger, a total stranger*; I also sensed

a doubt approaching me; perhaps I had been deluded
by my own passion, and I had always been a stranger to him.—
I flew out of their horrible house,
I left quickly before the memory of Myres should be
snatched away, should be altered by their Christianity.

IN THE SAME SPACE

The surroundings of the house, centers, neighborhoods
which I see and where I walk; for years and years.

I have created you in joy and in sorrows:
Out of so many circumstances, out of so many things.

You have become all feeling for me.

ALEXANDER JANNAIUS AND ALEXANDRA

Successful and entirely satisfied,
the King Alexander Jannaius
and his consort the Queen Alexandra,
preceded by a fanfare of music, pass with
all kinds of splendor and luxury
through the streets of Jerusalem.
The work undertaken by Judas Maccabaeus
and his four illustrious brothers,
and continued later with such dogged resolve,
amid perils and many difficulties,
has succeeded magnificently.
Now nothing inappropriate remains.
All submission to the arrogant monarchs
of Antioch has ceased. Look,
the King Alexander Jannaius
and his consort the Queen Alexandra
are equal in all to the Seleucids.
Good Jews, pure Jews, faithful Jews—above all.
But, as circumstances require it,
they are also masters of the Greek vernacular;
and they associate with Greeks and hellenized
monarchs—as equals, however, and that goes without saying.
The work undertaken by the great Judas Maccabaeus
and his four illustrious brothers
has truly succeeded magnificently,
has succeeded remarkably.

COME, O KING OF THE LACEDAEMONIANS

Cratesicleia did not condescend
to let the world see her weeping and mourning;
majestically she walked and in silence.
On her immobile face nothing was betrayed
of her extreme sorrow and her torment.
Nevertheless, for a moment, she did not hold back;
and before she embarked on the wretched ship for Alexandria,
she took her son to the temple of Poseidon,
and when they found themselves alone, she embraced him
and covered him with kisses, "in great pain," says
Plutarch, and "excessively troubled."
Nevertheless her strong character struggled;
and having recovered, the admirable woman
said to Cleomenes, "Come, O King of the
Lacedaemonians, when we go out of here,
let no person see us weep or conduct ourselves
in a manner that is unworthy of Sparta.
Let this remain between us alone;
as for our destiny, it will be according to god's will."

And she embarked on the ship, going toward that "will."

BEAUTIFUL FLOWERS AND WHITE THAT BECAME HIM WELL

He walked into the café where they used to go together.—
It was here that his friend had told him three months before,
"We haven't a farthing. We are two boys who are
completely penniless—reduced to the cheapest places.
I tell you this plainly, I can no longer go
around with you. Someone else, you must know, is asking for me."
This "someone else" had promised him two suits of clothes and a few
handkerchiefs made of silk.— To win him back once more
he moved heaven and earth, and he found twenty pounds.
He went around with him again because of the twenty pounds;
but also, along with these, for their old friendship,
for the old love they felt, for their very deep feeling.—
The "someone else" was a liar, a regular guttersnipe;
he had only one suit of clothes made for him, and
even that begrudgingly, after a thousand pleas.

But now he no longer wants either the suits of clothes,
or anything at all of the handkerchiefs of silk,
or the twenty pounds, or the twenty piasters.

On Sunday they buried him, at ten in the morning.
On Sunday they buried him, it is almost a week.

On his very cheap coffin, he placed flowers,
beautiful flowers and white that became him well,
that became his beauty and his twenty-two years.

In the evening when he went— on a job that came his way,
a need to earn his bread— to the café where they
used to go together: a knife in his heart,
was the desolate café where they used to go together.

HE ASKED ABOUT THE QUALITY

He came out of the office where he had been hired
in a menial and low-paying position,
(about eight pounds a month; gratuities included)
when the miserable work that had kept him
stooped all afternoon was over for the day,
he came out at seven o'clock and strolled slowly
and loitered on the street.— Handsome;
and interesting: so that he appeared to have arrived
at the full yield of his senses.
He passed his twenty-ninth birthday a month ago.

He loitered on the street, and in the poor
alleys leading to the dwelling where he lodged.

Passing in front of a little shop
where they sold cheap and shoddy
merchandise for laborers,
he saw a face inside, he saw a figure
that attracted him and he entered, pretending
he wanted to see some colored handkerchiefs.

He asked about the quality of the handkerchiefs,
and what they cost, in a choked voice
almost faded by longing.
And the answers came in the same vein,
distracted, in a low voice,
containing a latent consent.

They kept on finding something to say about the merchandise—
but their only aim: the touching of their hands
over the handkerchiefs; the coming close
of their faces, by chance their lips;
a momentary contact of the limbs.

Furtive and fleet, so that the storekeeper
who sat in the rear would not notice anything.

THEY SHOULD HAVE CARED

I am almost reduced to a vagrant and pauper.
This fatal city of Antioch
has consumed all my money;
this fatal city with its expensive life.

But I am young and in excellent health.
I possess a marvelous command of Greek
(I know Plato and Aristotle backward and forward,
what orators, what poets, and whoever you care to name).
I have an idea of military matters,
and I have friends among the mercenary chiefs.
I am a little on the inside of the administration too.
I spent six months in Alexandria, last year;
I know a thing or two (and that is useful) about things down there:
the views of Kakergetis, his villainies, et cetera.

So I consider myself fully qualified
and just the man to serve this nation,
my own beloved land of Syria.

In whatever position they place me
I will try to be useful to my land. This is my intention.
But if on the other hand they thwart me with their methods—
we know them, the diligent ones—need we talk about it now?
If they do thwart me, I am not to blame.

First of all I shall apply to Zabinas
and if that dolt does not appreciate me,
I will go to his opponent, to Grypos.
And if that idiot too does not engage me,
I will go directly to Hyrcanos.

At any rate, one of the three will want me.

As for my conscience, it is undisturbed
by the indifference of my choice.
All three of them are equally harmful to Syria.

But, a ruined man, why is it my fault?
Unfortunate me, I am trying to pull through.
The almighty gods should have cared
about creating a fourth man who was honest,
I would gladly have gone over to him.

THE MIRROR IN THE HALL

The wealthy home had in its entrance
an enormous, extremely old mirror,
that must have been bought at least eighty years ago.

An unusually handsome lad, a tailor's employee
(on Sundays an amateur athlete),
stood holding a parcel. He delivered it
to someone in the house, who carried it inside
to fetch the receipt. The tailor's employee
was left by himself, and he waited.
He approached the mirror and took a look at himself,
and he straightened his tie. Five minutes later
they brought back the receipt. He took it and left.

But the old mirror that had seen and seen,
during the long, long years of its existence,
thousands of objects and faces;
but this time the old mirror was delighted,
and it felt proud that it had received unto itself
for a few moments an image of flawless beauty.

ACCORDING TO ANCIENT FORMULAS OF GRECOSYRIAN MAGI

"What extract can be discovered from
witching herbs," said an aesthete,
"what extract prepared according to the
formulas of ancient Grecosyrian magi
that, for a day (if its potency
can last no longer), or even for an hour,
can evoke for me my twenty-three years;
can evoke again for me my friend
when he was twenty-two—his beauty, his love?

"What extract can be found according to the formulas
prepared by the ancient Grecosyrian magi which,
along with this return to the past,
can also evoke for me our little room?"

IN THE YEAR 200 B.C.

"Alexander, son of Philip, and the Greeks, except the Lacedaemonians . . ."

We can very easily imagine
how utterly indifferent they were in Sparta
to this inscription, "except the Lacedaemonians."
But it was natural. The Spartans were not
of those who would let themselves be led and ordered about
like highly paid servants. Besides,
a panhellenic campaign without
a Spartan king as commander in chief
would not have appeared very important.
O, most assuredly, "except the Lacedaemonians."

That too is a stand. It is understood.

So, except the Lacedaemonians, at Granicus;
and then at Issus; and in the decisive battle
where the formidable army that the Persians
had massed at Arbela was swept away,
that had set out from Arbela for victory and was swept away.

And out of the remarkable panhellenic campaign,
victorious, brilliant in every way,
celebrated far and wide, glorious
as no other had ever been glorified,
the incomparable: we were born;
a vast new Greek world, a great new Greek world.

We, the Alexandrians, the Antiocheans,
the Seleucians, and the innumerable
rest of the Greeks of Egypt and of Syria,
and of Media, and Persia, and the many others.
With our extensive empire,

with the varied action of our thoughtful adaptations,
and our common Greek, our Spoken Language,
we carried it into the heart of Bactria, to the Indians.

Are we going to talk of Lacedaemonians now!

DAYS OF 1908

That year he found himself out of work;
and so, he existed playing at cards
or backgammon; or on borrowed money.

A position, at three pounds a month, in a little
stationery store had been offered him.
But he refused it without any hesitation.
It didn't do. It was not the pay for him,
a young man with enough education, twenty-five years old.

He won or didn't win two or three shillings a day.
At cards and backgammon, what could the boy earn
in the cafés of his class, the popular ones,
though he played shrewdly, chose dunces for partners?
His borrowings, there were plenty, and more.
Rarely did he find a dollar, more often a half-dollar;
at times he was brought down to a shilling.

Some weeks, at times more often,
when he was spared the ghastly staying up at night,
he refreshed himself at the baths in a morning swim.

His clothes were appallingly shabby,
he always wore the same suit, a cinnamon-colored
suit that was pretty much faded.

O days of summer of nineteen hundred and eight,
from your image, for beauty's sake,
the faded cinnamon-colored suit is gone.
Your image has watched over him
when he took off, when he flung away from him
the worthless clothes and the mended underwear.
And he remained entirely naked; flawlessly handsome, a marvel.
His hair uncombed, standing up a little,
his limbs somewhat tanned by the sun,
by the morning nudity at the baths, at the beach.

IN THE SUBURBS OF ANTIOCH

We were bewildered at Antioch on learning
of the latest doings of Julian.

Apollo had it out with his highness at Daphne!
He would not give an oracle (as if we worried!),
he had no intention of speaking prophetically
until his temple at Daphne should first be purified.
The neighboring dead disturbed him, he said.

There were numerous graves at Daphne.
One of the dead who was buried there
was the marvelous, the glory of our church,
the saint, the victorious Martyr Babylas.

It was to him the false god alluded, the one he feared.
As long as he felt him near, he did not dare
to give out his oracles; he was mum.
(They are terrified of our martyrs, the false gods.)

The impious Julian rolled up his sleeves,
his nerves were on edge and he shouted: "Take him up, take him away.
Carry this Babylas away, at once.
Can you imagine? Apollo is annoyed.
Take him up, seize him immediately.
Unbury him, take him wherever you like.
Take him away, throw him out. Are we joking now?
Apollo said his temple had to be purified."

We took it, we carried the holy remains elsewhere,
we took it, we carried it with love and in honor.

And truly the temple showed beautiful improvement.
With no loss of time whatever,

a huge fire broke out: a raging fire:
and the temple was burnt and Apollo also.

The idol in ashes, to be swept away with the refuse.

Julian was bursting with rage and he spread it abroad—
what else was he to do?—that the fire had been started
by us Christians. Let him talk.
Nothing has been proved. Let him talk.
What really matters is that he was bursting with rage.

EARLY POEMS

Many if not all of Cavafy's early poems were published in magazines or almanacs during the period in which they were written, from 1886 through 1904. Later, Cavafy rejected his early poems and said that he did not wish them to appear in any collection of his work. They were therefore not included either in the original edition of the *Poems* published in Alexandria in 1935 under the supervision of his close friends Rika and Alexander Singopoulos or in the edition published in Athens in 1952.

During the past twenty-five years, however, all but two of the early poems have appeared in magazines or in biographies of Cavafy; as has so often happened in the past, the claim of posterity to all of the extant work of a great poet has asserted itself. In consideration of these facts, Mr. Singopoulos, the heir and literary executor of Cavafy, has consented to allow the publication of the early poems in this volume, where they appear for the first time in book form.

Cavafy is known to have written thirty-three, perhaps thirty-five early poems. Thirty-three of them, all that are available, appear here. The remaining two, despite extensive inquiry and research, have not been found.

For seventeen of the early poems I have used the texts as given in two issues of the mazagine *Ta Nea Grammata* (Athens), where they were published in 1936; the texts of thirteen of the poems were taken from *The Life and Work of Constantine Cavafy* by Michael Peridis. I have taken the texts of two of the poems from *Cavafy and His Epoch* by Stratis Tsirkas; and one is drawn from the magazine *Nea Estia* (Athens, 1942).

WHEN, MY FRIENDS, I WAS IN LOVE

. . . .

I had a lyrical fantasy,
and though it was deceitful,
yet it offered me happiness
that was lively and warm.

. . . .

And the cheap calico
dress that she wore,
I swear to you that at first,
it seemed to me like silk.

Two shoddy bracelets
adorned her arms;
for me they were jewels
of high nobility.

. . . .

The wit of orators or sages
does not persuade me now
as much as one nod of hers
did at that time.

. . . .

NTOUNIAN GKOUZEL

(YOUR LOVELY WORLD)

The mirror is not deceiving me, the image is true,
no other girl on earth is as beautiful as I.

. . . .

My body is graceful, they praise my foot,
my snow-white hands and neck, my silken hair . . .

. . . .

Had I been born Christian, I should be free
to show myself to all, by night and by day;
and admiring men, envious women,
seeing my beauty, both would confess, in agreement,
that nature will not produce another girl like me.
Every time I would pass in an open carriage,
the streets of Istanbul would be jammed with people
so that each would see me go by.

BACCHIC

Weary of the world's delusive instability,
I found quietness in my glass;
I enclose life and hope and desires within it;
give me to drink.

Here I feel far from misfortunes, the storms of life,
like a sailor who has been saved from a shipwreck,
and finds himself on a safe boat in harbor;
give me to drink.

O! health-giving heat of my wine, you take away
every chilling influence. Cold of envy or disgrace,
of hatred or intrigues does not touch me;
give me to drink.

I no longer see graceless truth naked.
I have enjoyed another life, and I have a new world;
I find myself in a wide meadow of dreams—
give, give me to drink!

And if it is a poison, and if I find in it
the bitterness of death, I still have found happiness,
delight, joy, and exaltation in the poison;
give me to drink!

A LOVE

(Adapted from a ballad, "Auld Robin Gray," written by the British poet Lady A. Barnard)

Misfortune does not lessen however much you speak of it.
But there are pains that will not stay quiet in the heart.
They thirst to get out and give vent to grieving.

Antony loved me and I loved him.
And he gave me his word he would not marry another!
But he was so poor and he was proud.
That is why he went and left on an ill-fated boat,
intending to find work, to learn a trade.
He wanted to become a seaman and a captain one day,
and then wed with his heart at peace.
Ah, a year had not passed and father falls
and breaks his leg and his right arm.
My mother fell ill. Whatever had been left us,
a bit of old copper, something of silver,
a few jewels my mother had saved,
were sold for a song.
Our calamity
became the village talk. They spread the news
in the big houses; and from his mansion
Stavros would come often to our house as friend
and protector . . . and he looked at me with love in his eyes.

My father was not working; my mother was not embroidering.
I toiled day and night, poured out my eyesight
and yet I could not earn their bread.
Stavros was rich and greathearted.
Simply—without boasting, without assuming—
and in secret he gave them the means and helped them to live
And my soul rejoiced for my poor parents—
and my soul wept for my poor self.
The unlucky day was not long in coming
when he stood close to me in the field and held

my hand and looked at me . . . I was trembling like a leaf
for I knew what he wanted and I did not love him . . .
The words faltered on his lips—until he said,
"Phroso, for their sakes won't you consent to marry me?"

"No," my heart cried out to me seeking Antony.
But the wild North Wind rose heavily,
and they were saying that he had gone down in strange seas.
Ah, how did the harsh poisoned lie come out! . . .
Ah, how can I live a wretch weeping night, day! . . .

My father said much to persuade me.
But my good mother said never a word to me,
she only looked into my eyes, and sorrow and poverty
flowed from her. I lost all courage.
I could not hold out. I gave him my hand.
My heart was buried deep in the sea.

All the village girls envied my fortune
for wedding a rich husband and a nobleman of means,
I a village girl, I a poor girl.

The village had never seen a grander wedding
than ours. Young, old gathered together
to see the lucky bride of the grand notable.
They strewed our road with lilies and with roses.
Dances and music everywhere, songs and feasts.
For me it was night. All wore black.

Only four months had passed since I married him,
and one night as I stood forlorn at the door of my house,
I see before me the shadow of Antony.
I thought it was a dream, I could not believe my eyes,
until he said, "My love why are you sad?
Our troubles are over, I have come to marry you."
Bitterly, bitterly, I welcomed him and told him all.

And I clasped his hands in mine as before,
and I kissed him as before and wept on his neck.
I told him that I loved no one but him . . .
I told him that they had deceived me, I believed
he had drowned in the storm . . . that only for the sake
of my mother, my father I had married . . .
That I preferred trials with him, poverty and scorn
to all the earth's riches brought by another . . .
I told him that I loved him as before, only now
my love is an unquenched fire that burns me,
now that I know that never, never, never
can he be mine and I his . . . And I told him
that if a little of the old love was left,
to swear never to see me again in his life . . .
I told him other, other things; things I cannot recall.
My head was burning. I was losing my mind.

But now all has ended. My life has gone black.
This world will have no more joy for me.
Would that death had carried me off! . . . But how can I die,
I have a heart-wound, but I am still young.

THE POET AND THE MUSE

THE POET

For what good purpose, what profit did destiny seek,
was it in my frailty that I was created a poet?
My words are unavailing; the sounds of my harp,
even the most musical ones, are not true.

Should I want to hymn noble sentiments,
glory and virtue, I feel, are dreams.
I find discouragement everywhere I look,
and everywhere my foot slips on thorns.

The earth is a benighted sphere, cold and crafty.
My songs are a beguiling image of the world.
I sing of love and joy. Miserable parody,
miserable harp, a prey to all sorts of cheats!

THE MUSE

You are not a liar, poet. The world you vision
is the true one. Only the chords of the harp
know truth, and in this life,
they alone are our sure guides.

You are the priest of the divine. It gave you the lot
of beauty and the spring. Mellifluous song
drops from your lips, and you are a treasury of myrrh—
golden promise and a voice from on high.

If the earth is veiled in darkness, have no fear.
Do not think it is a perpetual darkness.
Friend, you are close to pleasures, flowers, valleys;
have courage, and step forward. Behold the early dawn!

It is only a light mist that frightens your vision.
Under the veil, gracious nature prepares for you
garlands of roses and violets and noble narcissus,
sweet-scented rewards for your songs.

BUILDERS

Progress is a tremendous edifice,—each carries
his stone; one carries words, others counsel, another
deeds—and day by day it raises its head
higher. Should a hurricane, a sudden swell

come, the good workers rush together
in a throng and defend their lost work.
Lost, because each one's life is expended
suffering abuse, pains, for a future generation,

that this generation may know honest happiness
and long life and riches and wisdom,
without base sweat or servile work.

But this fabled generation will never, never live.
This work will be wrecked by its very perfection
and all their vain toil will begin anew.

THE WORD AND SILENCE

If words have no meaning, silence is precious.
Arabian proverb

Silence is golden and the word is silver.

What profane one pronounced such blasphemy?
What sluggish Asian blind and mute resigned to
blind mute destiny? What wretched madman,
a stranger to humanity, insulting virtue
called the soul a chimera and the word silver?
Our only god-befitting gift, containing all—
enthusiasm, sorrow, joy, love;
our only human trait in our bestial nature!
You who call it silver do not have faith
in the future that will dissolve silence, mysterious word.
You do not luxuriate in wisdom, progress does not charm you;
with ignorance—golden silence—you are pleased.
You are ill. Unfeeling Silence is a grave disease;
while the warm, sympathetic Word is health.
Silence is shadow and night, the Word is daylight.
The Word is truth, life, immortality.
Let us speak, let us speak—silence does not suit us
since we have been created in the image of the Word.
Let us speak, let us speak—since within us speaks
divine thought, the soul's unbodied speech.

SHAM-EL-NESSIM

(BREATHING THE BREEZE)

Our pallid Egypt
the sun scorches and scourges
with bitter- and spite-laden arrows
and exhausts it with thirst and disease.
Our sweet Egypt
in a gay fair
gets drunk, forgets, and adorns itself, and rejoices
and scorns the tyrannical sun.

Joyous Sham-el-Nessim, innocent country festival,
announces the spring.
Alexandria with her many dense roads empties.
The good Egyptian wants to celebrate
the joyous Sham-el-Nessim and he becomes a nomad.
From everywhere pour out

the battalions of holiday lovers. The Khabari fills
and the blue-green, musing Mahmoudiya.
The Mex, Muharram Bey, the Ramleh are jammed.
And the countrysides compete to see which will get
the most carts, loaded with happy people, arriving
in solemn, serene merriment.

For the Egyptian preserves his solemnity
even at the festival;
he adorns his fez with flowers but his face
is immobile. He murmurs a monotonous song
with gaiety. There is much good spirit in his thoughts,
least in his movements.

Our Egypt has no rich greenness,
no delightful creeks or fountains,

it has no high mountains that cast a broad shade.
But it has magic flowers fallen aflame
from the torch of Ptah; exhaling unknown fragrance,
 aromas in which nature swoons.

Amid a circle of admirers the sweet singer of the
 widest fame is warmly applauded;
in his tremulous voice pains of love
sigh; his song bitterly complains
of the fickle Fatma or cruel Emineh,
 of the wiliest Zeinab.

With the shaded tents and the cold sherbet,
 the scorching heat and dust are routed.
The hours pass like moments, like steeds hastening
over the smooth plain and their gleaming manes
fanning out gaily over the festival
 gild the joyous Sham-el-Nessim.

 Our pallid Egypt
 the sun scorches and scourges
with bitter- and spite-laden arrows
and exhausts it with thirst and disease.
 Our sweet Egypt
 in a gay festival
gets drunk, forgets, and adorns itself, and rejoices
and scorns the tyrannical sun.

SINGER

Far from the world, poetic magic intoxicates him;
for him beautiful verses are the whole world.
Fantasy has built for her songster
a strong house of the spirit that destiny cannot shake.

You may say, "Life is cold and futile. It is folly
to think that life consists of the pleasant
sounds of a flute, and nothing else." Or, "Hard insensibility
lashes the one who was never wracked by the pain

of the struggle of life." But your judgment
is delusion and injustice. His Nature is divine.
Judge not in your logical, blind sickness.

The walls of his house are of magic emerald—
and voices within them whisper, "Friend, be quiet;
meditate and sing. Be of good heart, mystic apostle!"

VULNERANT OMNES ULTIMA NECAT

The metropolis of Bruges, which a mighty
Flemish duke once built and lavishly dowered,
has a clock with silver portals
that has been telling time for many ages.

The Clock said, "My life is cold,
        and colorless and cruel.
For me each day on earth is the same.
Friday and Saturday, Sunday, Monday,
are no different. I live—without hoping;
my only amusement, my only diversion
in my destined bitter monotony,
        is the world's destruction.
As I turn my hands sluggishly, languidly,
the delusion of everything earthly appears before me.
End and fall everywhere. Dins of unassailable strife,
groans buzz around me—and I conclude that
each of my hours wounds; the last one slays."

The Archpriest heard the audacious word
and said, "Clock, this language grates against
your ecclesiastical, your lofty rank.
How did such an evil thought creep
into your mind? O foolish, heretical idea!
        For a long boredom
has filled your mind with a dense mist.
        The chorus of hours
received another mission from the Lord
Each one rekindles; the last one begets."

GOOD AND BAD WEATHER

It does not bother me if outside
winter spreads fog, clouds, and cold.
Spring is within me, true joy.
Laughter is a sun ray, all pure gold,
there is no other garden like love,
the warmth of song melts all the snows.

What good is it that outside spring
sends up flowers and sows greenness!
I have winter within me when the heart hurts.
The sigh blots out the most brilliant sun;
if you have sorrow May resembles December,
tears are colder than the cold snow.

ELEGY OF THE FLOWERS

The loveliest flowers blossom in the spring.
And youth seems lovelier than all the flowers
of the field. But it withers early
and once it goes, it does not come again;
jasmine sprinkles it with the tears of dew.

The loveliest flowers blossom in the summer.
But the same eyes do not look at them.
And other hands place them on other breasts.
The same months come, but they look different;
the faces have changed and they do not recognize them.

The loveliest flowers blossom in the summer.
But they do not always stay with our joy.
They delight us, and they also embitter us;
and they grow among graves where we weep,
even as they color our laughing fields.

Summer has returned and the fields blossom anew.
But from the window it is hard to reach.
The windowpane grows smaller—smaller, fades.
The pained eye grows misty, is caught,
our heavy tired feet do not carry us.

For us this year no fields will blossom anew.
The roses of forgotten August wreathe us,
our former years swiftly return,
beloved shadows sweetly beckon us,
and lull our poor heart to deep slumber.

MELANCHOLY HOURS

The fortunate ones profane nature.
Earth is a sanctuary of sorrow.
Dawn drops a tear of unknown pain;
the wan orphan evenings mourn
and the select soul intones sadly.

I hear sighs in zephyr breezes.
I see sadness on the violets.
I feel the painful life of the rose;
the meadows alive with mysterious sorrow;
and within the dense forest echoes a sob.

People honor the fortunate ones
and poetasters sing hymns to them.
But Nature's portals are closed
to all those who indifferently, callously deride,
aliens who deride in an unfortunate land.

TO THE MOON

(Adapted from Shelley's "To the Moon.")

Have you grown pale out of the
boredom of ascending to heaven
and gazing earthward,
roaming around without a companion
among distant alien stars?
Your perennial changing is like
a joyless compassionless eye
that finds no worthy constancy.

THE INKWELL

Honest inkwell, sacred to the poet,
whence a whole world emerges,
as each figure draws near you,
it returns with a new kind of grace.

Where did your ink discover such fabulous
wealth! As each of its drops falls
on the paper it sets one more diamond
among the diamonds of our fantasy.

Who taught you the words that you launch
into the world's midst, and they fire us?
Even our children's children will read them
with the same feeling and warmth.

Where did you find these words that though they echo
in our ears as if heard for the first time,
yet do not appear entirely strange—
our hearts must have known them in another life.

The pen you moisten resembles a hand
moving around the clock of the soul.
It counts and determines the moments of feeling,
it counts and changes the hours of the soul.

Honest inkwell, sacred to the poet,
from whose ink a world emerges—
now comes to mind how many people
will be lost in it if deep sleep

should overtake the poet some night.
The words will always be there; but what strange hand
will be able to find them, bring them to us?
You, faithful to the poet, will refuse it.

ATHENA'S VOTE

Whenever justice is bereft of solution,
whenever the judgment of men is in doubt
and needs superior help and enlightenment,
the judges become sickly silent, small,
and the compassion of the gods decides.

Pallas said to the people of Athens,
"I founded your court. Neither Greece
nor any other state will ever acquire
a more glorious one. Honorable judges,
prove deserving of it. Renounce
improper passions. Let mercy
accompany justice. If your judgment
be stern then let it also be pure—
as pure as an unblemished diamond.
Let your work be a guide and a rule for prudence,
for benevolent and magnanimous deeds,
never foolish vengeance."

The citizens replied with feeling,
"Oh Goddess, our minds cannot find
adequate tribute of gratitude
for your splendid benefaction."

The gray-eyed
goddess replied, "Mortals,
divinity requests no wages of you.
Be virtuous and unbiased.
This suffices me. Besides, honorable judges,
I have guarded my own right of a single vote."

The judges said, "You who reside
in the starry firmament, Goddess,
how is it you vote here, with us?"

"Let not this
curiosity grieve you. I am restrained
in the use of my vote. But should the moment
occur when you are divided into two factions,
one for, the other against, you yourselves
will make use of my vote, without my leaving
the rooms of heaven. Citizens, I desire
that clemency should always be shown
to the accused. In the soul
of your Athena dwells great
limitless, ancestral forgiveness,
an instinct from Metis, the crown
of supremest wisdom in the heavens."

TIMOLAOS THE SYRACUSAN

Timolaos is the first musician
of the first city of Sicily.
The Greeks of our Western Greece,
from Naples and Marseilles,
from Taranto, Reggio, Agrigento,
and from as many other cities on the shores
of Hesperia that they crown with hellenism,
hasten in eager throngs to Syracuse,
to hear the glorious musician.
Most wise in the lyre and the cithara,
he also knows the delicate three-hole flute,
tenderest of tender flutes. He produces
a plaintive melody from the reed.
And whenever he takes his harp
in his hands, its chords give out poetry
of torrid Asia—initiation
of voluptuousness and sweet musing,
fragrance of Ecbatana and Nineveh.

. . . .

. . . .

But amid the multitudinous praises,
amid the gifts worth many talents,
the good Timolaos is very sad.
Robust Samos wine does not gladden him;
by his silence he insults the symposium.
Some indistinct sorrow possesses him,
the sorrow of his great frailty.
He feels that his organs within him are hollow,
while his soul is filled with music.
With diligence, with perseverance, he strives
in vain to pour out his secret notes;
his most perfect harmonies remain
mute and latent within him.

The enthusiastic throngs admire
everything he blames and scorns.
The loud voice of the praises disturbs him,
and amid the gifts worth many talents
the musician stands distracted.

OEDIPUS

Written after reading the description of the painting "Oedipus and the Sphinx" by Gustav Moreau.

The Sphinx is fallen on him,
with teeth and talons outspread
and with all the furor of life.
Oedipus succumbed to her first impulse;
her first appearance terrified him—
such a face, and such talk
till then he had never imagined.
But though the monster rests
her two paws on Oedipus' breast
he has recovered quickly—and now
he no longer fears her for he has
the solution ready and he will win.
And yet he does not rejoice over this victory.
His glance, full of melancholy,
is not on the Sphinx; far off he sees
the narrow path that leads to Thebes
and will end at Colonus.
And his soul clearly forebodes
that there the Sphinx will accost him again
with more difficult and more baffling
enigmas that have no answer.

BY THE OPEN WINDOW

In the calm of the autumn night
I sit by the open window
For whole hours in perfect
Delightful quietness.
The light rain of leaves falls.
The sigh of the corruptible world
Echoes in my corruptible nature.
But it is a sweet sigh, it soars as a prayer.
My window opens up a world
Unknown. A source of ineffable,
Perfumed memories is offered me;
Wings beat at my window—
Refreshing autumnal spirits
Come unto me and encircle me
And they speak with me in their innocent tongue.
I feel indistinct, far-reaching hopes
And in the venerable silence
Of creation, my ears hear melodies,
They hear crystalline, mystical
Music from the chorus of the stars.

ODE AND ELEGY OF THE ROADS

The walk of the first pedestrian,
the lively shout of the first vendor,
the opening of the first windows,
of the first door—is the ode
the roads have in the morning.

The footsteps of the last pedestrian,
the shout of the last vendor,
the shutting of the doors and the windows—
is the voice of the elegy
the roads have in the evening.

IN THE HOUSE OF THE SOUL

Deeper, at the very depths, in the House of the Soul
Passions go and come and sit around the fire with their
faces of women. GEORGES RODENBACH

Desires saunter in the House of the Soul—
lovely ladies silken-gowned
and sapphire-crowned.
They command all the halls of the House from the door
to the depths. In the largest hall—
on nights when their blood is ardent—
they dance and drink with loosened hair.

Outside the halls, pale and shabbily dressed
in the clothes of olden days,
the Virtues pace about and listen in bitterness
to the carousal of the drunken Hetaerae.
Faces are glued to windowpanes
and silently, in deep thought they gaze,
at the lights, the jewels, and the flowers of the dance.

THERE IS A BLESSED JOY

But there is a blessed joy
a consolation in this sorrow.
How many multitudes of vulgar days
how much boredom are spared this end!

A poet said, "That music is beloved
that cannot be sounded."
And I think that the choicest life
is the life that cannot be lived.

OUR DEAREST WHITE YOUTH

Our dearest, our white youth,
ah, our white, our snow-white youth,
that is infinite, and yet so brief,
spreads over us like the wings of an archangel! . . .
It is forever exhausted, forever loving;
and it melts and faints among white horizons.
Ah, it goes there, is lost in white horizons,
goes forever.

Forever, no. It will return,
it will come back, it will return.
With its white limbs, its white grace,
our white youth will come and take us.
It will seize us with its white hands,
and with a thin shroud drawn from its whiteness,
a snow-white shroud drawn from its whiteness,
it will cover us.

ADDITION

I do not question whether I am happy or not.
But one thing I always keep gladly in mind;
that in the great addition—their addition that I abhor—
that has so many numbers, I am not one
of the many units there. I was not counted
in the total sum. And this joy suffices me.

THE BANK OF THE FUTURE

To make my arduous life secure
I will issue very few drafts
on the Bank of the Future.

I doubt if it has a large capital.
And I have begun to fear that at the first crisis
it will suddenly stop its payments.

DEATH OF THE EMPEROR TACITUS

Emperor Tacitus is ill.
His deep old age was unable to withstand
the toils of war.
He is bedridden in the hateful camp,
in wretched Tyana—so far away!—

He remembers his beloved Campania,
his garden, his villa, his morning
stroll—his life six months before.
And in his agony he curses
the Senate, the detestable Senate.

THE TEARS OF PHAETON'S SISTERS

Like light in matter, like diaphanous
gold, is precious amber.—
When an awful, frantic power
envying Phaeton hurled him headlong

from the pinnacle of heaven,
his sisters came dressed in mourning
to the watery grave of Eridanus
and day, night, the wretched ones wept.

And all mortals lamented with them
the vanity of soaring dreams.
O pitiless fortune, O hateful destiny,
Phaeton fell headlong from the clouds.

Within our humble hearths
let us live lowly and contented with little;
let us drive out the yearnings from our hearts,
let every bent heavenward cease.

The wretched ones were forever weeping,
Phaeton's sisters were weeping,
and in each of the folds of the Eridanus,
their pale faces were mirrored.

Moved to the extreme, the earth
received and treasured the reverend tears
of the sisters. But as seven days went by
and the eighth dawn brightened

their many, many weepings
gave way to eternal brilliance
and were transformed into lustrous amber.
O choice stone! O good tears!

Noble lamentation, envied lament,
full of love and full of sparkle—
honorable sisters with tears of light,
you wept for the finest young man on earth.

ANCIENT TRAGEDY

Ancient tragedy, ancient tragedy
is as holy and wide as the universal heart.
A demos gave birth to it, one city in Greece,
but quickly it soared and set the stage in heaven.
In an Olympian theater, an arena worthy of them,
Hippolytus, Ajax, Alcestis, and Clytemnestra
tell us of life, woeful and empty,
and the drop of divine mercy falls on the pained earth.
The people of Athens saw and admired
tragedy in its youngest form.
Tragedy flourished within the sapphire
theater of heaven. There its listeners were
the immortals. And the gods in great seats
of pure diamond heard in inexpressible
gladness the beautiful verses of Sophocles,
the throbs of Euripides, the majesty of Aeschylus
and the Attic fantasy of the subtle Agathon.
The Muses, Hermes, and the wise Apollo,
the beloved Dionysus, Athene, and Hebe,
were the worthy actors of the sublime dramas.
And the vaults of heaven were filled with poetry,
the monologues resound, eloquent and mournful;
and the choruses, inexhaustible sources of harmony;
and the witty dialogue with its succinct phrases.
All nature is reverently silent, lest the noise
of the tempest disturb the divine holiday.
Motionless and reverent, the air, the earth, and the sea
guarded the tranquillity of the great gods.
And sometimes an echo from on high came to them,
an ethereal bouquet of a few verses breathed
"Well done, well done," the blended trimeters of the gods.
And the air kept saying to the earth and the aged earth to the sea:
"Silence, silence, let us hear. Within the heavenly theater
they are giving a performance of Antigone."

Ancient tragedy, ancient tragedy
is as holy and wide as the universal heart.
A demos gave birth to it, one city in Greece,
but quickly it soared and set the stage in heaven.

In the Olympian theater, in an arena worthy of them,
Hippolytus, Ajax, Alcestis, and Clytemnestra
tell us of life, woeful and empty.
And the drop of divine mercy falls on the pained earth.

HORACE IN ATHENS

In the room of Leah the hetaera
where elegance, wealth, a soft bed are found,
a young man with jasmine in his hands is talking.
Many stones adorn his fingers,

and he wears a himation of white silk
with red oriental embroidery.
His language is Attic and pure,
but a slight accent in his pronunciation

betrays his Tiber and Latium origin.
The young man confesses his love
and the Athenian girl hears him in silence,
listens to Horace, her eloquent lover.

And dazzled she sees new worlds of Beauty
in the passion of the great Italian.

THE TARANTINIANS CAROUSE

The theaters are full, music everywhere;
here debauchery and lewdness, and there
athletic and sophistical contests.
An unwithering wreath adorns the statue
of Dionysus. Not an earthly nook remains
unsprinkled by libations. The citizens of Taranto carouse.

But the Senators withdraw from all this
and sullen they say many things in anger.
And each barbarian toga fleeing
looks like a cloud threatening a storm.

VOICE FROM THE SEA

The sea gives out a secret voice—
    a voice that enters
our heart, and moves it,
    and delights it.

The sea intones for us a tender song,
a song composed by three great poets,
    the sun, the air, and the sky.
She intones it with that divine voice of hers,
when summer weather spreads calm
    like a gown over her shoulders.

Her melody wafts dewy messages
to souls. She recalls the youthful past
without rancor and without pining.
The loves of the past speak in secret,
forgotten sentiments again come to life
within the sweet breathing of the waves.

The sea intones for us a tender song,
a song composed by three great poets,
    the sun, the air, and the sky.
And as you look at her watery meadow,
as you see her infinite greenness,
her field that is so near and yet so far,

covered with yellow flowers that the light sows
like a gardener, joy takes hold of you,
    and it intoxicates you, lifts up your heart.
And if you are young, the longing for the sea
will run through your veins; out of its love
the wave will say a word to you; it will water
    your love with a secret fragrance.

The sea gives out a secret voice—
a voice that enters
our heart, and moves it,
and delights it.

Is it a song or a plaint of the drowned?—
the tragic plaint of the dead
who have the cold foam as their shroud,
and they weep for their wives, for their children,
for their parents, for their desolate nest,
as the bitter sea lashes them.

It pushes them against crags and jagged rocks,
it tangles them among the weeds, pulls them in, pushes them out;
and they run as if they were alive,
with terrified, wide-open eyes,
and with their hands wild and stretched out rigid,
from their last agony.

Is it a song or a plaint of the drowned?—
the tragic plaint of the dead
who are pining for a Christian cemetery.
A grave, that relatives sprinkle with tears,
and loving hands adorn with flowers,
and where the sun pours warm, compassionate light.

A grave, that the immaculate cross guards,
where sometimes some priest will go
to burn incense and say a prayer,
a widow brings him in remembrance of her husband
or a son, or sometimes a grieving friend.
They commemorate the dead one; and the soul
forgiven rests more peacefully.

INTERVENTION OF THE GODS

Remonin— . . . He will disappear at the right moment;
the gods will intervene.
Mme de Rumieres— As in the ancient tragedies?
(Act II, Scene 1)
Mme de R.— What's the matter?
R.— The gods have arrived.
(Act V, Scene 10)
DUMAS FILS, *The Strange Woman*

Heartily knows
. . . .
The gods arrive.
EMERSON, "Give All to Love"

Now this will be done and then that;
and later on, in a year or two—as I reckon—
actions will be thus and so, manners will be thus and so.
We will not try for a far-off hereafter.
We will try for the best.
And the more we try, the more we will spoil,
we will complicate matters till we find ourselves
in utter confusion. And then we will stop.
It will be the hour for the gods to work.
The gods always come. They will come down
from their machines, and some they will save,
others they will lift forcibly, abruptly
by the middle; and when they bring some order
they will retire. And then this one will do one thing,
that one another; and in time the others
will do their things. And we will start over again.

ARTIFICIAL FLOWERS

I do not want the real narcissus—nor do lilies
please me, nor real roses.
They adorn the trite, pedestrian gardens.
Their flesh embitters, tires, and pains me—
I am weary of their perishable beauties.

Give me artificial flowers—glories of glass and metal—
with never-wilting, never-spoiling, never-aging forms.
Flowers of superb gardens of another land
where Contemplations and Rhythms and Learning dwell.

I love flowers fashioned of glass or gold,
genuine gifts of a genuine Art,
dyed in hues lovelier than natural colors
wrought with mother-of-pearl and enamel,
with ideal leaves and stalks.

They draw their grace from wise and purest Taste.
They did not sprout unclean in dirt and mire.
If they have no aroma, we will pour fragrance,
we will burn myrrh of sentiment before them.

BIOGRAPHICAL NOTE BY RAE DALVEN

Konstantinos P. Kabaphēs, or Constantine P. Cavafy, as he is generally known in the non-Greek world today, was the son of Peter John Cavafy and Chariclea Photiady, both of well-to-do families in Constantinople. Peter John and his elder brother, George, on the death of their father in 1842, became partners in the family firm, Cavafy and Sons. And in 1850, Peter John migrated with his young wife and their first child to Alexandria to establish a branch of the firm in that city. They had eight more children, of whom one son and the only daughter died in infancy. Constantine, their youngest son, was born on April 17, 1863.

In Constantinople, Cavafy and Sons was a manufacturing firm. In Alexandria, Peter John turned it into an export house dealing in grain, cotton, and raw buffalo skins. Meanwhile, George had left Constantinople, to settle in England. There he set up branches of Cavafy and Sons in Liverpool, Manchester, and London, which handled the products exported from Egypt by Peter John. In 1855, the manufacturing firm in Constantinople was discontinued, and henceforth the two brothers devoted their attention almost exclusively to the growing trade in Egyptian cotton. According to the "Genealogy" which the poet compiled in 1911 and which is the source of many of the facts here cited, Cavafy and Sons eventually became one of the largest commercial houses of its kind in Egypt, where it had four branches. It was one of the first companies to introduce the cotton gin in Egypt, and in 1869, Ismail Pasha decorated Peter John in recognition of his services to the development of industry in his adopted country.

Peter John was a generous contributor to the Greek community in Alexandria and prominent in its religious and commercial life. But he was also European in his outlook, and his friends and associates, who were often entertained in his home, included not only his Greek compatriots, but also the industrialists and professional men, the people of substance and distinction, and of various nationalities, who made up the aristocracy of Alexandria.

Such was the world that Constantine knew in his earliest years in the house on fashionable Seriph Pasha Street where he was born. Then, in 1870, when he was seven, his father died, leaving "very little," according to the "Genealogy," because he had "lived big" to maintain his position. Two years later, Chariclea took her brood to England, and the family remained there for the next seven years. In 1877, the firm of Cavafy and Sons was dissolved, and in 1879 Chariclea returned to Alexandria with six of her sons; George, the eldest, chose to remain in London.

The five older sons took positions in Alexandria. Chariclea enrolled her youngest "Anglo-Greek," who was now sixteen, in a "lyceum of business practice" called the Hermes, perhaps because three of his childhood friends attended it. Little is known about Constantine's education up to this time, but in the "Genealogy" he says that he was tutored at home in French and English, and he was probably tutored in other subjects as well. He was brought up in the Greek Orthodox religion, though nothing is known about the strictness, or lack of it, in his family's observance of their faith.

At the Hermes, the subject to which Constantine applied himself most diligently had nothing to do with commerce. K. Papatzis, director of the lyceum, happened to be an ardent classicist. He found his pupil a willing student and he inspired in the boy so deep a love for the classics and for ancient Greek civilization that Constantine, when he was old enough, became a Greek citizen.

In June, 1882, an anti-foreign, anti-Christian outbreak caused the murder of many Europeans and resulted in the British bombardment of the Alexandrian forts. The city was in flames. Most of the foreign communities fled to the foreign warships which were already in the harbor. Chariclea and her sons went to Constantinople to the home of her father, George Photiady, a dealer in diamonds. A few months later, when things had settled down, the five older sons returned to Alexandria, where they resumed their occupations, but Chariclea and Constantine spent the next three years in Constantinople.

Chariclea, unlike Peter John, came of a long line of Phanariots, those Greeks who became powerful in clerical or other offices under Turkish patronage. (The name derives from the Phanar, a quarter of the city that became the chief Greek quarter.)

In the home of his grandfather, whom he came to love and admire, Constantine became familiar with the history of his maternal forebears, their distinctions, and their contributions to the Greek community, and he often spoke with pride of his Phanariot ancestry. He also came to know the leaders of the Phanariot community, who were his grandfather's friends and associates. During the three years he spent in Constantinople, he applied himself to the study of Byzantine and Hellenic history, which became a lifelong interest and from which the subject matter of so many of his poems is drawn. He also continued his study of languages; he first read Dante in the original at this time. And he wrote his first poems.

It was during his stay in Constantinople, too, that he became interested in demotic Greek—the language spoken by the common people of Greece. He read the *Erotokritos,* a long poem in the demotic written by Vincenzo Kornaros about 1650; he became familiar with the Greek folk songs that have come down through the centuries by word of mouth. He also read modern Greek poetry, written both in the purist and the demotic. In particular, he studied the poetry of Dionysios

Solomos, the Italian-educated poet who turned, in his writing, to the demotic Greek he had learned as a child and who later became the national poet of Greece.

In honor of George Photiady, Constantine added the middle initial Ph. to his name in 1882, and retained it until 1896, the year of his grandfather's death. From 1896 to 1899, he used no middle initial. Then he added his father's initial, P., and thereafter signed himself Konstantinos P. Kabaphēs. In the non-Greek world, he is sometimes referred to as Cavafis, but his friends among non-Greeks as well as the three closest Greek friends of his youth with whom he corresponded in English addressed him as Constantine P. Cavafy—which seems to have been the choice of the poet himself.

Chariclea and Constantine returned to Alexandria in 1885. It is not known whether George Photiady helped his daughter financially, but Constantine's brothers were able to help their mother, and it is known that the poet's second oldest brother, Peter, who wished Constantine to go on with his writing, contributed most to his support. For the next seven years, Constantine continued to devote his time to study and writing. He read ever more widely in Byzantine and Hellenic history and literature; he particularly admired the ancient Byzantine and Alexandrian Epigrammatists, Simonides of Ceos, Callimachus, Meleager, and Lucian. His interest in demotic Greek led him to the linguistic studies of Yiannis Psiharis, who ridiculed the purist and argued for an uncompromising adoption of the demotic as the only hope for Greek literature and for the cultural development of the Greek people. And during these years he read extensively in Latin, French, and English literature.

The Alexandria to which Cavafy returned had gone through a series of distressing upheavals of which the British bombardment in 1882 had been only the beginning. Egypt was now practically a dependency of England. The commercial life of the Greek community had been destroyed, and Alexandrian Greeks found it difficult to rebuild their life and their institutions in a time of general misery and decadence. As Stratis Tsirkas, Cavafy's most recent biographer, puts it, "The moral and material countenance of Egypt which the Cavafy family knew was disfigured." Cavafy never took part in any political activity, but he was liberal and humanistic in his thought. The conditions he found distressed him, and some of his early poems, written during this period, reflect his pessimism.

In 1891, Constantine's brother Peter died, and the poet decided to earn his own living. On March 1, 1892, when he was not quite twenty-nine, he went to work as a provisional clerk in the Ministry of Irrigation. He could never expect to receive a permanent appointment because he was a Greek citizen. Nevertheless, he chose to remain at the Ministry, and he continued as a provisional clerk for thirty years, until his retirement in 1922. Tsirkas and Michael Peridis, his biographers, both say that Chariclea, with whom he lived, supplemented his meager salary with monthly gifts. And for a few years he earned extra money as a broker on the Alexandria stock exchange. From the poet's file at the Ministry, which Tsirkas reproduces, we learn that he was found "most useful" because of his extensive knowledge of languages. Eventually, he knew, besides ancient and modern Greek, English, French, Italian, Latin, and Arabic. Perhaps it was for this reason that he was allowed whole afternoons off to attend to his business as a broker.

It was about 1895 that Cavafy met Pericles Anastasiades, seven years younger than himself, who became and remained his close friend. Anastasiades, who had been raised and educated in England, was a cultivated man and had a talent for painting. The two shared a love for French literature and for the literature and civilization of England. Anastasiades was a great admirer of Cavafy's poetry, and Cavafy trusted him both as a friend and as a critic. Not long after the beginning of their friendship, the poet began sending to Anastasiades copies of poems and notes and critical comments on literature, writers, and contemporary events, most of them handwritten on scraps of paper. Anastasiades preserved the poems and the notes, and his collection, now known as the Anastasiades Archive, is of great value to the student of Cavafy. It includes, incidentally, a sheaf of twenty poems translated into English by Constantine's brother John.

Credit must also be given to Anastasiades for hastening Cavafy's recognition in Greece. In 1901, Anastasiades gave Constantine a hundred pounds, with which the poet made his first trip to Athens. There he met the well-known novelist Gregory Xenopoulos and various magazine editors to whom he showed his poems. In 1903, when Cavafy was again in Athens, Xenopoulos selected twelve of the poems Cavafy had given him and had them published in the magazine *Panatheneum* along with an article on Cavafy's work.

On February 4, 1899, Cavafy's mother, Chariclea, with whom he had always lived and to whom he was a devoted son, died suddenly of a heart attack. Her death was only the beginning of a "somber line" of family deaths and separations which occurred within a few years. In August, 1900, Constantine's eldest brother, George, who had returned from London with a fatal illness, died. His brother Aristedes, who had moved to Cairo, died in 1902. In 1903, Alexander, the brother Constantine loved best, died in Athens, where the poet had accompanied him in search of expert medical attention. In 1906, his brother John, with whom he had lived since his mother's death and who, more than any of his brothers, understood his work, moved to Cairo, and returned to Alexandria only in the year of his death, 1923. From 1906 to 1908, Constantine lived with Paul, the only brother still remaining in Alexandria. But in 1908, Paul migrated to Paris, where he remained until his death in 1920. It was after Paul's departure that Cavafy took the apartment at 10 Lepsius Street where he lived alone for the rest of his days.

Cavafy is said to have written about seventy poems a year. Of these, however, he saved only four or five and destroyed the rest. Occasionally, he sent poems to almanacs or magazines, but he preferred another, indirect way of testing the merit of his work. According to Timos Malanos, his first Alexandrian biographer, Cavafy had a pathological fear of the opinion of the public. His practice was to send copies of his work to his friends, and only after the praise of his friends had convinced him of the worth of his poems did he offer them for publication. He published his first book in 1904—when he was forty-one—and it contained only fourteen poems. He did not send copies to the critics; but the book did not go unnoticed, and critics began to write and even to lecture about his work.

In 1907, Cavafy became interested in a youth group, the Nea Zoe (New Life), which was dedicated to literature and the advancement of demotic Greek and which published a magazine called *Nea Zoe*. Cavafy was too old to become a member of the group, but he attended its meetings regularly and became one of the magazine's most valued contributors. He came to speak of himself as a demoticist; as Peridis says, "Cavafy had a fighting linguistic conscience, and he spoke often of the phenomena and the problems of the demotic language." But he also appreciated the beauties of the traditional literary language. Purist Greek was part of his heritage, and he never renounced the language of his family and his class. Instead, he used both the purist and the demotic, and one of the great distinctions of his poetry lies in its subtle and sensitive combining of the two.

In 1910, he published his second collection, adding twelve poems to the fourteen included in the first book. *Nea Zoe* published his poems steadily from 1908 to 1918. *Ta Grammata,* another Alexandrian magazine, founded in 1911, also published much of his work. As the years passed, his poems were published more and more widely in Greece, and his work began to be translated into French, Italian, German, and English. But he published no more books during his lifetime, and the first comprehensive edition of his poems, which did not include his early work, was published in 1935, two years after his death.

Pericles Anastasiades had much to do with making Cavafy's work known in the non-Greek world, and it was Anastasiades who introduced

Cavafy to the novelist E. M. Forster. This was during World War I, when Forster, having volunteered for the Red Cross, was stationed in Alexandria. Forster, who became Cavafy's good friend, introduced his work to T. S. Eliot, Arnold Toynbee, and D. H. Lawrence, among others. The second edition of Forster's *Alexandria: A History and a Guide* (1938) was dedicated to Cavafy, and his book *Pharos and Pharillon*, published in 1923, contains an evocative and amusing essay on the poet. In 1949, on the sixteenth anniversary of Cavafy's death, Forster wrote to Anastasiades: "I often think of my good fortune and the opportunity, which the chance of a horrible war gave me, to meet one of the great poets of our time."

In *Pharos and Pharillon* there is a short passage that vividly summons up the poet.

> . . . a Greek gentleman in a straw hat, standing absolutely motionless at a slight angle to the universe. His arms are extended, possibly. "Oh, Cavafy . . . !" Yes, it is Mr. Cavafy, and he is going either from his flat to the office, or from his office to the flat. If the former, he vanishes when seen, with a slight gesture of despair. If the latter, he may be prevailed upon to begin a sentence—an immense complicated yet shapely sentence, full of parentheses that never get mixed and of reservations that really do reserve; a sentence that moves with logic to its foreseen end, yet to an end that is always more vivid and thrilling than one foresaw. Sometimes the sentence is finished in the street, sometimes the traffic murders it, sometimes it lasts into the flat. It deals with the tricky behaviour of the Emperor Alexius Comnenus in 1096, or with olives, their possibilities and price, or with the fortunes of friends, or with George Eliot, or the dialects of the interior of Asia Minor. It is delivered with equal ease in Greek, English, or French. And despite its intellectual richness and human outlook, despite the matured charity of its judgments, one feels that it too stands at a slight angle to the universe: it is the sentence of a poet.

After his retirement from the Ministry of Irrigation in 1922, Cavafy spent his days with his books and his writing. Friends came to see him, and sometimes visitors from other countries. Michael Peridis, who often visited him at 10 Lepsius Street, tells us that his apartment consisted of a long hallway, lined with books, a living room occupying the width of the house, with a large sofa and other furniture that was Arabian in style, and a bedroom which was also the study. "There was another room which Mr. Sarejiannis [an Alexandrian Greek writer] called the 'book bindery.' . . . Candlelight and beautiful petroleum lamps contributed to the great distinction of the apartment, but there was a deeper distinction in the personality of its tenant that made it unique in the whole city."

In the evening, Cavafy would stroll to the neighborhood café, where a group of friends and admirers always awaited him, to sip Turkish coffee with him and to listen to the "organ cadence" of his voice. A place was made for him at the center of the group, and if they had started a discussion before he came, they went back to its beginning. The talk might be of poetry or history or contemporary events. Sometimes he talked about his own work, and G. Lechonitis, in his unpublished notes, "Kabaphika Autoscholia" (literally, "Cavafian Selfnotes"), quotes his remarks on one such occasion:

> Many poets are exclusively poets. . . . I, I am a poet-historian. I, I could never write a novel or a play, but I feel in me a hundred and twenty-five voices that tell me that I could write history. But now there is no more time.

In June, 1932, Cavafy showed signs of cancer of the throat but refused to accept the doctor's diagnosis. His condition worsened, and his close friends Rika and Alexander Singopoulos persuaded him to go to Athens to consult doctors there. He entered the Red Cross Hospital in Athens on July 4, and a tracheotomy was immediately performed. The operation was successful, but it resulted in the complete loss of his voice. He returned to Alexandria in October. Early in 1933, he suffered a relapse and was taken to the Greek hospital of Alexandria, where he spent the last months of his life. Sarejiannis, in an article published in the Athenian magazine *Ta Nea Grammata* in 1944, notes that a few days before Cavafy's death, the Patriarch of Alexandria was summoned to administer Holy Communion. Cavafy had not been consulted, and when the prelate was announced, he "refused, was enraged, persisted . . ." In the end, however, he submitted and received communion but "with compunction." He died on April 29, and was buried the next day in the family plot in the cemetery of the Greek community in Alexandria.

In 1948, the Pnevmatiki Estia (Cultural Hearth) of Alexandria, of which Timos Malanos was the head, placed a commemorative plaque on the wall of the house at 10 Lepsius Street.

The most interesting as well as the most controversial element in Cavafy's poetry is his unique mixture of purist and demotic Greek. There were riots in Athens in 1901 (the so-called "Gospel riots") when Alexander Pallis's translation of the New Testament in the demotic appeared serially in the daily newspaper *Acropolis.* In 1903, another riot broke out because of the presentation in the demotic of the trilogy of Aeschylus. The demotic language was not officially recognized by the state until 1917. Not until then was it taught in the schools.

Since that time, however, the gap between the demotic and the purist has narrowed considerably. Purist phrases, words, and grammatical constructions have now become part of the spoken language. Purist expressions like *ἐν πάσῃ περιπτώσει* (in any case, in any event), *πλήν* (but), *ἐν μέρει* (in part); purist spellings of verbs like *ξεύρω* (I know) and *ἔλθω* (I come) and of nouns like *υἱός* (son) and *ὑαλί* (glass); nouns with purist endings like *ἐργάται* (workers) and *νομοθέται* (lawmakers); the *ν* endings of purist accusative nouns and adjectives and purist *ς* endings—all of these are to be heard on the streets and read in the daily newspapers of Greece today.

Conversely, more and more demotic phrases, words, and constructions have found their way into the purist. The staunchest supporter of the purist uses the demotic for bread, which is *ψωμί,* instead of the purist *ἄρτος,* and this in spite of the fact that he goes to an *ἀρτοπωλεῖον* (breadseller) to buy bread. He uses the demotic for wine, *κρασί,* instead of the purist *οἶνος,* although the purist form is familiar to the common people. At the shoe store he asks for *παπούτσια* instead of *ὑποδήματα.*

A letter Cavafy wrote in English to Pericles Anastasiades about 1896 suggests how deeply he thought about the language of his poems. Referring to an article he had written, he says, "I am rather satisfied with its diction, over which I have taken many pains. I have tried to blend the spoken with the written language and have called to my help, in the process . . . all my experience and as much artistic insight as I possess in the matter—trembling, so to speak, for every word."

The poet's first consideration was not whether an expression or a construction was purist or demotic, but whether it served his poetic purpose. For instance, in the poem "Supplication" (1898), which is mainly in the demotic, he used the purist spelling of icon, *εἰκών,* instead of the demotic, *εἰκόνα,* probably because he was speaking of the Virgin Mary and the traditional spelling seemed more appropriate. In "The Funeral of Sarpedon" (1899), in the lines

μὲ μαργαριταρένιο
χτένι κτενίζει τὰ κατάμαυρα μαλλιά

he uses the demotic spelling *χτένι* for the noun *comb* and the purist spelling for the verb to *comb* *κτενίζει* because, we may assume, the two χ sounds so near each other would be inharmonious. In "Expecting the Barbarians" (1900), he uses the purist construction *νομοθετήσουν* (pass laws) in one line and the demotic construction of the same verb, *νομοθετοῦνε*, in another; in the same poem he uses the purist *αὐτοκράτωρ* (monarch) in one line and the demotic *αὐτοκράτορας* in another. In "Morning Sea" (1915), he uses the purist *ἰνδάλματα* (vision, image) because there is no demotic word that carries the nuance of the purist word. Sometimes his choice of a word has to do with rhythm, as when he uses the purist *ὅπου* (when) instead of the demotic *πού* because he needs another syllable. In the title of "The God Forsakes Antony," which is taken from Plutarch, he uses the same form of the verb that Plutarch used—*ἀπολείπειν* (forsakes).

Most of Cavafy's early poems are a blend of the purist and "a decent demotic that is timid and lacks experience," as Peridis puts it. The poems in the main body of his work are in the demotic except for occasional purist words and constructions.

In his earliest poems, Cavafy used all kinds of metrical feet, but after 1900 he used only the iambic in lines ranging from six to eighteen and in one instance nineteen syllables. In only three poems are the lines all the same length. Thus, "The First Step" (1900) is written entirely in lines of eleven syllables, "Infidelity" (1901) in lines of thirteen syllables, "The Tomb of Lánes" (1918) in lines of fifteen syllables. The larger portion of his work is written in lines of eleven to sixteen syllables. Cavafy boasted that no single poem of his resembled another in this respect.

The Greek language is inflected, and every Greek word carries an accent—with the exception that an enclitic, if it is a monosyllable and follows a word that is accented on the last syllable, is governed by the accent of the word on which it depends and is not itself accented.

In the Greek iambic, the stress must always fall on the accented syllable of a polysyllabic word, but it may also fall on other syllables as it would in pronunciation; the stress may not fall on prepositions, conjunctions, articles, and pronouns, when these are monosyllables, because they are indeclinable, and there should be a correlation between accented words and stresses in a line of a given length. The feminine ending is acceptable, and the first foot of a line may be a trochaic.

In general, Cavafy follows the rules, but he allows himself a certain freedom. Let us look at the first four lines of "Che Fece . . . Il Gran Rifiuto." The first line is a pure iambic line of thirteen syllables with a feminine ending.

Σὲ μερικοὺς ἀνθρώπους ἔρχεται μιὰ μέρα

The fourth, sixth, eighth, and twelfth stresses are on accented syllables, as they should be in a line of thirteen syllables. The line begins with an accented word, but the word is a preposition. The second line is also a pure iambic line of fifteen syllables, again with a feminine ending.

ποὺ πρέπει τὸ μεγάλο Ναί, ἤ τὸ μεγάλο τὸ Ὄχι

In this line all of the stresses fall on accented syllables. Two of the stresses, however, fall on the word τὸ, which is an article ("the"), perhaps because Cavafy wishes to emphasize "*the* great Yes" and "*the* great No." Again, the first word carries an accent, but it is a pronoun. The last two words are contracted. The third line is another regular fifteen-syllable iambic—in which the last stress falls, by the way, on the same syllable (but of a different word) that he has used, in the second line, in a visually contracted form.

νὰ ποῦνε φανερώνεται ἀμέσως ὅποις τὄχει

In the fourth line of fifteen syllables,

Ἕτοιμο μέσα του τὸ Ναὶ καὶ λέγοντας τὸ πέρα

the first foot is trochaic and again there is a feminine ending. (The third word is an enclitic and therefore carries no accent.) In this line the word "the" before Yes and No is not stressed.

Cavafy's stanzas vary greatly in length and arrangement as the thought and feeling of the poem dictate. The stanza is in itself a poetic device.

In eighteen of the poems, Cavafy breaks his lines visually. He uses this device in a variety of ways and for various reasons—to break the monotony, to create a satirical effect, to sustain the rhythmic flow of the verse, to give the poem a conversational tone. In "In the Month of Athyr" (1917), he varies the effect of the lines by letting the metrical foot run over from one hemistich to the next. All of the lines are end-stopped; the position of the break is varied from line to line. In "An Artisan of Wine-Mixing Bowls" (1921) he adds in line seven a dash after a period. In the poem "In Despair" (1923), he introduces two dashes in the first hemistich of the second line of the second stanza to create an effect of poignancy.

For he wanted—so he said— he wanted to be saved.

In the last line of the same stanza, he uses a dash at the end of the first hemistich and breaks the second with an internal dash:

There was still time— as he said—to be saved.

Cavafy gave much thought to phonic values. In "Voices" (1894), where the poet is submitting to something far off and nostalgic, nine of the fourteen vowels are short i's. In the ninth line of "Footsteps" (1900), where the cowardliness of the Lares is the main feeling he wishes to convey, seven of the eight vowels are short. In "The City" (1917), Cavafy selects words with many consonants because, as Peridis points out, he wanted words that harmonized with "the majesty of the picture he portrayed."

Cavafy makes effective use of repetition—to heighten the feeling, to give a sense of finality, to unify, to create a dramatic effect. In "Orophernes" (1915), the first and last stanzas open and close with the same line, and the repetition conveys a sense of inevitability and tragedy as the poet reflects on a wasted life. Repetition adds a meditative note to the poem "In the Evening" (1917):

An echo of the days of pleasure,
an echo of the days drew near me.

And in "For Ammonis, Who Died at 29 in 610," repetition intensifies the sense of loss.

Our sorrow and love pass into a foreign tongue.
Pour your Egyptian feeling into a foreign tongue.

In the poem "The Ides of March" (1911) repetition adds to the sense of urgency as the poet advises Caesar

do not fail to stop; do not fail to put off
all talk or work; do not fail to turn away. . . .

Cavafy is a master of the run-on line, but he uses it sparingly. He uses feminine and masculine endings in all possible combinations. He often uses synizesis. In "Ithaca" (1911), three words are contracted into one: δώσει ἡ 'Ιθάκη. In "Chandelier" (1914), Cavafy contracts an article and a noun: ἡ ἡδονή; there are three contractions in "In Harbor" (1918) γιὰ οἰκίαν, ποιὰ ἡ πατρίς, ποιοί ἦσαν; two in "The Tomb of Lánes" (1918) ποὺ ἀγάπησες, ποὺ ἔρχεσαι. And there is one in "Sophist Leaving Syria" (1926) πιὸ εὐειδής.

Fifty-five of Cavafy's poems are wholly in rhyme, and the rhyme patterns are of a great variety. In "The City" (1894), the first and last lines of each octet rhyme; the lines between are rhymed couplets. There are alternate rhymes in "Walls" (1896) and "Monotony" (1908). In "An Old Man" (1898), the last line of each tercet rhymes with the last line of the next, while the first two lines of each tercet are a rhymed couplet. In "He Is the Man" (1909), the first line rhymes with the tenth and last line, the second with the ninth, the third with the eighth, and so on; and in this poem, incidentally, the lines that rhyme have the same number of syllables. "The Battle of Magnesia" (1915) and "Julian in Nicomedeia" (1924) are in rhymed couplets.

Many other poems are partly in rhyme, and the rhymes are distributed with great ingenuity. For instance, in the poem "In Despair" (1923), which consists of two sets of hemistichs, the rhyme scheme for the first set is aabcd adeef aghc, for the second, ccich jcccc jkcb. In "In the Month of Athyr" (1917), the first and eighth lines of the first set of hemistichs rhyme. In the second set, Cavafy ends the third, fifth, and eleventh lines with the same word; the tenth line ends with another word, but one that rhymes with these three.

In translating the main body of the poems by C. P. Cavafy, I have used the text of the *Poems* published in Athens in 1952 by the Ikaros Publishing Company. The text of this edition is the same as that of the first edition of the *Poems* published in Alexandria by Henōsis Hellenōn Logotehnōn (Society of Hellenic Men of Letters) in 1935 under the supervision of Cavafy's close friends Rika and Alexander Singopoulos.

As Mr. Auden points out in his Introduction, there is, in English, nothing comparable to the purist and the demotic in Greek. Therefore it is impossible for a translator to represent Cavafy's blending of the two. I have tried, however, to preserve the effect of his language. This language is informal and idiomatic—modern Greek as it was used by educated Alexandrian Greeks in Cavafy's time. His language is economical. Every word is carefully chosen, and indispensable.

Because many Greek words are longer than their English equivalents, it is not always possible to keep the same number of syllables in a line without adding words or syllables. But to give any effect of padding would be to violate the spirit of the original. In a good many instances, therefore, the line in English is somewhat shorter than the line in Greek.

As I have already pointed out, many of Cavafy's poems are wholly or partly in rhyme. I have not attempted to preserve the rhyme. In the notes for the individual poems, I have indicated which of them are wholly in rhyme and I have also set down the rhyme scheme for each of these.

For the rest, the translations are as close to the original as I could make them. In this connection, perhaps I should note that Cavafy's grammar is not always perfect. Given the care with which he composed his poems, we may assume that these "errors" are for the most part deliberate. At any rate, they are Cavafy's. Likewise, the occasional sudden shifts in tense are Cavafy's, not mine. As for punctuation, I have taken a few liberties with commas; other marks—for instance, a dash after a period—which may seem odd, have been retained because Cavafy used them.

DESIRES. In rhyme, abcacb.

VOICES. An early version of this poem which appeared in the *Egyptian Almanac* in 1895 was entitled "Sweet Voices" and consisted of four tercets written in alternate rhymes. In its final form, it is in free verse.

SUPPLICATION. In homophonous rhymes, aa bb cc dd.

THE FIRST STEP. Theocritus (c. 310-c. 245 B.C.), one of the most renowned poets of the Hellenistic era, was born in Syracuse. He visited Alexandria in 273 B.C. in the reign of Ptolemy Philadelphus. He is most famous for his pastoral lyrics.

AN OLD MAN. In rhyme, aab ccb dde ffe ggh iih.

CANDLES. Cavafy, who spoke of this poem as "one of the best things I ever wrote," is often called "the poet of the Candles."

THERMOPYLAE. Ephialtes was the Greek who betrayed the defenders of Thermopylae to the Persians. See Herodotus, V, 39–41; VII, 202–205; and IX, 10.

CHE FECE . . . IL GRAN RIFIUTO. In rhyme, abba cddc. The title is taken from line 60, Canto 3, of Dante's *Inferno*. The line in full reads, "*che fece per viltate il gran rifiuto*" (who made through cowardice the great refusal). It refers to Celestine, who was elected pope in 1294. Cavafy's interpretation is that Celestine abdicated out of humility and high scruples. Hence his omission, in the title, of the phrase "*per viltate*." Celestine was canonized by Clement V in 1313.

THE SOULS OF OLD MEN. In rhyme, abbccdda.

INTERRUPTION. In rhyme, aabccbdd. Metaneira, queen of Eleusis, engaged Demeter, who was disguised as an old woman, as a wet nurse for her newborn son Demophoon. Demeter decided to make the child immortal and held him over the fire to burn away his mortality. She was interrupted by Metaneira, who snatched the child away before the process was complete. The sea nymph Thetis was likewise burning away the mortality of her son Achilles when she was interrupted by her husband King Peleus. See "Homeric Hymn to Demeter."

THE WINDOWS. In rhyme, aabcddcb.

FOOTSTEPS. The early version of this poem was entitled "The Footsteps of the Eumenides" and consisted of fifteen lines instead of the present nineteen. It was inspired by Suetonius, *Life of Nero*, XLVI.

MONOTONY. In rhyme, abab cdcd.

WALLS. In homophonous rhymes, ab ab cd cd.

THE FUNERAL OF SARPEDON. Sarpedon was the son of Zeus and Laodameia and king of the Lycians, who were allies of the Trojans. He was killed by Patroclus, son of Menoetius, intimate friend of Achilles. Phoebus Apollo was Sarpedon's stepbrother. Adapted from the *Iliad,* XVI, 462–501, 666–684.

DIONYSUS AND HIS CREW. In rhymed couplets. Ácratos, Méthe, Hedýoinos, Mólpos, Hedymelés, Cómus, and Teleté are the divinities of License, Drunkenness, Wine, Tune, Song, Mirth, and Revelry.

THE HORSES OF ACHILLES. In rhyme, abbccddaaee fgghhiiffee. The two immortal horses sired by Zephyr (West Wind) and the harpy Podargē were named Balius and Xanthē. Adapted from the *Iliad,* XVI, 149–154, and XVII, 426–447.

HE IS THE MAN. In rhyme, abc deed cba. See Lucian's "The Dream" (*Lucian,* Loeb Classics, Vol. 3, p. 224).

KING DEMETRIUS. Demetrius, King of Macedonia (337–283 B.C.) and stepbrother of Alexander the Great, was hailed as Poliorcetes (Besieger) and Sôtêr (Savior). He was later expelled by the combined forces of Pyrrhus and Lysimachus. Cavafy differs from Plutarch in his interpretation of the final attitude of the King when he was defeated. Pyrrhus was king of Epirus in 306 and from 295 until his death in 272 B.C. The subject of the Cavafy poem is taken from Plutarch's "Life of Demetrius," Chapters XLIV and XLI, and Lucian's Dialogue "The Cock" (*Lucian,* Loeb Classics, Vol. 2, p. 227).

THE CITY. In rhyme, abbccdda effggdde. Originally entitled "In the Same City." Cavafy sent an autographed copy to his friend Pericles Anastasiades along with a letter written in English which reads as follows: "It is from one point of view perfect. The versification and chiefly the rhymes are faultless. Out of the seven rhymes on which this poem is built, three are identical in sound and one has the accent on the antepenultimate. But I have *παρακάμει* [overdone] it and somehow got cramped on the exigencies of the meter; and I am afraid I haven't put in the second stanza as much as should have gone into it. I am not sure that I have drawn in the 2nd 3rd and 4th lines of the second stanza an adequately powerful image of ennui —as my purpose was. It may be however that by trying to do more, I should have overdone the effect and strained the sentiment, both fatal accidents in art. There is a class of poems whose role is 'suggestif.' My poem comes under that head. To a sympathetic reader —sympathetic by culture—who will think over the poem for a minute or two, my lines, I am convinced, will suggest an image of the deep, the endless 'desésperance' which they contain 'yet cannot all reveal.' " Cavafy kept "The City" in his drawer for fifteen years, making changes in it until 1909, when it was printed in the magazine *Nea Zoe*. He did not include it, however, in the collection of 1910.

THE IDES OF MARCH. Artemidorus was a teacher of Greek philosophy at Rome and a friend of Caesar. See Plutarch's "Life of Julius Caesar" and Shakespeare's *Julius Caesar*, also Suetonius, "Julius Caesar," LXXXI.

THE GOD FORSAKES ANTONY. The god is Bacchus, protector of Antony. The poem refers to Plutarch's story that before the fall of Alexandria and his own death, Antony heard "the sound of all sorts of instruments, and voices singing in tune, and the cry of a crowd of people, shouting and dancing, like a troop of bacchanals on its way. This tumultuous procession seemed to take its course right through the middle of the city to the gate nearest the enemy; here it became the loudest, and suddenly passed out. People who reflected considered this to signify that Bacchus, the god whom Antony had always made it his study to copy and imitate, had now forsaken him" (Plutarch's "Life of Antony," p. 1147). See also Shakespeare's *Antony and Cleopatra*, Act IV, Scene 3.

IONIAN SONG. The poem is a reworking of an earlier one entitled "Memory."

PERILOUS THINGS. Augustus Constans, Roman Emperor from A.D. 337 to 350, was the youngest son of Constantine the Great. He became emperor, together with his brothers Constantine and Constantius in 337, on the death of their father. In 340, war broke out among the brothers, and Constantine was killed. Constans then also ruled his brother's dominions. He was killed by a soldier in 350.

THE GLORY OF THE PTOLEMIES. In rhyme, abbacccc. The Ptolemies were sixteen kings of Egypt forming the Macedonian Dynasty, which ruled from 323 to 30 B.C. The Ptolemy referred to in this poem is Ptolemy I Sôtêr (Savior) (c. 367–283 B.C.). He became king of Egypt in 323 and ruled until 285 B.C., when he abdicated in favor of his son Ptolemy II. Seleucus, surnamed Nicator (c. 358–280 B.C.) was the founder of the Seleucid Dynasty in Syria.

HEROD OF ATTICA. Herod of Attica (A.D. 101–177) was a renowned sophist in Athens. Alexander of Seleucia was derisively known as the "clay Plato." See Philostratus, *Lives of the Sophists*, II, B. 1–15 and E, I. See also H. J. Rose, *Handbook of Greek Literature*, and Aulus Gellius, *Noctes Atticae*, XIX. 12.

PHILHELLENE. In this poem, a puppet monarch of the Seleucid kingdom is ordering his coinage. Edwyn Bevan writes in his book *House of*

Seleucus (Vol. II, p. 159): "The money of the Kingdom of Parthia was stamped exclusively with Greek legends and from the time of Mithridates I they commonly added to their other surnames that of 'Philhellene.'"

ALEXANDRIAN KINGS. Caesarion was supposed to be the son of Julius Caesar and Cleopatra. Alexander and Ptolemy were Antony's sons. Antony himself conferred the honors on the three children. See Plutarch's "Life of Antony," LIV, and Shakespeare's *Antony and Cleopatra*, Act III, Scene 6.

IN CHURCH. The hexapteriga is a sacred standard used in the Greek Orthodox Church. It has a six-winged cherub in a sunburst at its center. It stands behind the holy altar except when it is used in processions.

OF THE SHOP. Homophonous rhymes, aa bb cc dd ee.

THE GRAVE OF THE GRAMMARIAN LYSIAS. In rhyme, abacbbcb.

FAR OFF. In rhyme except for one line, abc deed.

THE GRAVE OF EURION. In rhyme, abcaddefebcbf.

CHANDELIER. In rhyme, abaac dbddc.

THEODOTUS. Theodotus, according to Plutarch, was a "hired teacher of rhetoric from Chios who brought to Caesar the head and signet ring of Pompey." See Plutarch's "Life of Pompey."

BUT WISE MEN PERCEIVE APPROACHING THINGS. In rhyme, abcab dbcdc.

OROPHERNES. See Edwyn Bevan's *House of Seleucus*, Vol. II, pp. 157, 159, 205–209. See also Athenaeus, X, 440 B.

ON PAINTING. In rhyme, abbcadeccedb.

THE BATTLE OF MAGNESIA. In rhymed couplets. Antiochus the Great, King of Syria from 223 to 187 B.C., was defeated by the Romans at the Battle of Magnesia in 190 B.C. Philip V, the last king of Macedonia of that name, had been defeated by the Romans at Kynoskefalai (Cynoscephalae) seven years earlier.

MANUEL COMNENUS. Manuel I Comnenus was emperor of Byzantium from A.D. 1143 to 1180. *Kyr* means sire.

THE DISPLEASURE OF THE SON OF SELEUCUS. Demetrius Sôtêr was the son of Seleucus IV Philopator, and the grandson of Antiochus the Great. He reigned in Syria from 162 to 150 B.C. During the reign of his father, Demetrius was sent to Rome as a hostage. The Ptolemy referred to is Ptolemy VI Philometor, who reigned from 181 to 145 B.C. See Edwyn Bevan, Vol. 2, p. 189.

BEFORE THE STATUE OF ENDYMION. In rhyme, abbabccac.

TOMB OF IASES. In rhyme, abab cdcd.

PASSAGE. In rhyme, except for one line; aabbccdeebb.

IN THE MONTH OF ATHYR. In the ancient Egyptian calendar, Athyr was the third month, corresponding to the period between October 10 and November 8. KZ (Kappa Zeta) are the Greek numerals for 27.

CAESARION. Caesarion appears also in "Alexandrian Kings." He was assassinated by the Romans in 30 B.C., after the defeat of Antony.

IN HARBOR. In rhyme, aabbccddaeae. The tenio is a timber tree found in southern South America. Its wood is rosy brown in color.

NERO'S TERM. See Suetonius, *Life of Nero,* XL.

ENVOYS FROM ALEXANDRIA. In rhymed couplets. The quarrel between Ptolemy VI Philometor, and his younger brother Ptolemy VII, Euergetes II, took place in 164 B.C. and was arbitrated at Rome. The scene at Delphi was invented by Cavafy. See note on "The Displeasure of the Son of Seleucus," above.

ARISTOBOULUS. Cypris was Herod's mother, and Salome his sister. Alexandra was the mother of Herod's wife Mariamne and of Aristoboulus. See *The Works of Flavius Josephus,* pp. 454–455.

IMENUS. Michael III (A.D. 839–867), surnamed the Drunkard, was a Byzantine emperor. In 867, he was assassinated by Basil the Macedonian.

OF DEMETRIUS SÔTÊR, 162–150 B.C. See notes to "Orophernes" and "The Displeasure of the Son of Seleucus," above. See also Edwyn Bevan, *House of Seleucus,* Vol. 2, p. 188, and Polybius, XXXI, 12.

IF DEAD INDEED. Apollonius of Tyana was a mystical philosopher who came from Asia Minor in the region north of the island of Cyprus. Philostratus (A.D. c. 170–245) studied and taught in Athens, then proceeded to Rome, where he met Empress Julia Domna, who gave him the memoirs and labors of Apollonius. Under her urging, Philostratus undertook to write his biography. These memoirs were attributed to a certain Damis, a native of Nineveh, who had been a disciple and companion of Apollonius. Justin I was East Roman Emperor from A.D. 518 to 527. In 519, he effected a reconciliation of the Eastern and Western Churches. See *Life of Apollonius* by Philostratus.

ANNA COMNENA. Only the first two lines are rhymed. Anna Comnena (A.D. 1083–1148), Byzantine historian who described herself as "born and bred in the purple," was the oldest daughter of Alexius and Irene, Emperor and Empress of the East. She wrote the *Alexiad,* a history of her father's achievements, consisting of fifteen books covering the period from 1069 to 1118. See Chapter 4 of the Prologue to the *Alexiad.*

YOUNG MEN OF SIDON (A.D. 400). See *Aeschylus,* ed. by Nicolaus Wecklein, 495; *Aeschylus,* Loeb Classics, Vol. 2, "Epigrams," No. 272, p. 520. See also J. W. Mackail's *Select Epigrams from the Greek An-*

thology, p. 50. Datis was a Median general who with Artaphernes, nephew of Darius, commanded the army of Darius I which was defeated in 490 B.C. at Marathon by the Athenians.

FAVOR OF ALEXANDER BALAS. In rhyme, ababcccdd. Alexander Balas pretended to be the son of Antiochus Epiphanes and heir to the Syrian throne. He overthrew Demetrius I Sôtêr in 150 B.C. and made himself king of Syria. In 146 B.C., the son of Demetrius Sôtêr defeated him in a battle near Antioch. He fled for refuge to a prince, who murdered him.

DEMARATUS. Demaratus was king of Sparta from 510 to 491 B.C. After Demaratus was deposed, Leotichides received the kingdom. See Herodotus, Books VI and VII.

FROM THE SCHOOL OF THE RENOWNED PHILOSOPHER. Ammonius Saccas was a Neoplatonic philosopher who taught in Alexandria in the third century A.D.

TO ANTIOCHUS EPIPHANES. Antiochus Epiphanes was king of Syria from 175 to 163 B.C. His father, Antiochus the Great (223–187 B.C.), was defeated by the Romans at Magnesia. His brother Seleucus Philopator was assassinated in 175. The daughter of Seleucus was the wife of Perseus, last king of Macedonia, who was defeated by the Romans at Pydna in 168 B.C. Antiochus Epiphanes is known for his infamous persecutions of the Jews which led to the Maccabean revolt.

THOSE WHO FOUGHT FOR THE ACHAEAN LEAGUE. Daos and Critolaus, generals of the Achaean League, were both defeated in 146 B.C. at Corinth by Mummius. Ptolemy VIII Lathyrus (also called Philometor) reigned over Egypt and Cyprus in association with his daughter Berenice.

EPITAPH OF ANTIOCHUS, KING OF COMMAGENE. Antiochus I, King of Commagene, reigned in the latter half of the first century B.C.

JULIAN SEEING INDIFFERENCE. Julian, called the Apostate, Roman emperor from A.D. 361 to 363, was attracted to paganism and the philosophy of the ancient Greek world. The opening quotation is taken from one of his letters to Theodorus (*Julian*, Loeb Classics, Vol. 3, letter 20, p. 59).

JULIAN IN NICOMEDEIA. In rhymed couplets. Julian the Apostate had to conceal his anti-Christian beliefs before he became emperor. Gallus was Julian's brother who was executed by the Emperor Constantius in A.D. 354. Maximus of Ephesus, a Neoplatonic philosopher, was one of Julian's teachers. Mardonius was his tutor from the time he was seven years old. See Julian's *Misopôgôn* (*Julian*, Loeb Classics, Vol. 2, p. 460).

IN ALEXANDRIA, 31 B.C. In rhymed couplets.

JOHN CANTACUZENUS TRIUMPHS. John VI (c. 1292–1383) was a Byzantine emperor and historian. Under Andronicus III, who reigned from c. 1328 to 1341, he had principal charge of the government, and when Andronicus died, he became regent, since the new emperor, John Paleologus, was only nine years old. During his temporary absence from Istanbul, the Dowager Empress, Anne of Savoy, confiscated his property and imprisoned some of the members of his family. Upon his return, Cantacuzenus revolted and proclaimed himself emperor. After six years of civil war, during which the empire was impoverished and nearly destroyed, Cantacuzenus became joint emperor with John Paleologus, but monopolized the royal power. Eventually, he was forced to abdicate. He entered a monastery, where he wrote his memoirs, which cover the period from 1320 to 1327. *Kyr* and *Kyria* mean Sire and Lady. Kyria Irene was the wife of John Cantacuzenus.

BY AN ITALIAN SHORE. Corinth was pillaged and destroyed by Mummius in 146 B.C.

OF COLORED GLASS. The coronation of John Cantacuzenus and Irene Asan took place at the Blachernae Palace in Constantinople. The incident is taken from *The Roman History* of Nicephorus Gregoras, Byzantine historian (1295–1360). See Volume 2. Andronicus Asan was also a great feudal lord. See note on "John Cantacuzenus Triumphs," above.

TEMETHOS OF ANTIOCH, A.D. 400. The Syrians referred to the dynasty of the Seleucids as the "Kingdom of the Greeks." See note on "To Antiochus Epiphanes," above.

APOLLONIUS OF TYANA IN RHODES. This young man in Rhodes had spent an enormous sum of money building a luxurious home but had spent nothing on his education. The incident is taken from the *Life of Apollonius* by Philostratus, Book V, Chapter 22. See note on "If Dead Indeed," above.

IN A TOWNSHIP OF ASIA MINOR. See note on "In Alexandria, 31 B.C.," above.

A GREAT PROCESSION OF PRIESTS AND LAYMEN. Julian was mortally wounded by an arrow in the war with the Persians, A.D. 363. Jovian was unexpectedly proclaimed his successor by the army. He continued the retreat begun by Julian, but had to make a humiliating treaty with the Persians. On his way back to Istanbul, he caught cold and was found dead in his bed. During his short reign, he succeeded in rescinding the edicts of Julian against the Christians but granted protection to those who chose to remain pagans. See Julian's *Misopôgôn* (*Julian*, Loeb Classics, Vol. 2, p. 486).

PRIEST AT THE SERAPEUM. The temple of Serapis in Alexandria was destroyed during the persecution of the pagans initiated by the Emperor Theodosius in A.D. 392.

ANNA DALASSENÉ. In rhyme, aabcddbc. The royal edict in which Alexius I Comnenus appointed his mother regent of the empire is quoted by his daughter Anna Comnena in the *Alexiad*, Book III, Chapter 6.

GREEK SINCE ANCIENT TIMES. Io, daughter of Inachus, King of Argus, was changed into a heifer by Zeus because of Hera's jealousy. After her many wanderings, she was restored to her original form in Egypt. Her brothers, in her honor, built a city named Iopolis, on the site on which Seleucus Nicator, the Macedonian, founded the Syrian capital. The Antiocheans commemorated this ancient connection with Hellenic Argus.

IN A FAMOUS GREEK COLONY, 200 B.C. In rhyme, except for one line; aabbc aaddceef ghfghhhii jjf abakc balalb.

UNDERSTOOD NOT. The words "I recognized, I read, I condemned" will be found in the letters of Julian the Apostate. See *Julian*, Loeb Classics, Vol. 3, letter 81 to Basil, p. 286.

IN SPARTA. Cleomenes III, King of Sparta, son and successor of Leonidus II, reigned from about 235 to 219 B.C. His plans to raise Sparta to the position of leadership in Greece caused war between Sparta and the Achaean League in 227 B.C. The incident is taken from Plutarch's "Life of Agis and Cleomenes," XXII.

ON THE MARCH TO SINOPE. The "noble companion" is Demetrius, who as a young man was the friend of the future Mithridates II. Demetrius, having been told under a vow of silence that Mithridates' father planned to execute him, traced on the earth, as his friend looked on, "Flee Mithridates." The Mithridates of the poem was assassinated at Sinope. Demetrius became king of Macedonia in 294 B.C.

ALEXANDER JANNAIUS AND ALEXANDRA. Alexander Jannaius of the house of Maccabaeus reigned as king of the Jews at Jerusalem from 103 to 76 B.C.

COME, O KING OF THE LACEDAEMONIANS. See Plutarch's "Life of Cleomenes," XXII.

THEY SHOULD HAVE CARED. Cavafy calls Ptolemy, surnamed Euergetes (Benefactor) II and nicknamed Ptolemy Physcon (bloated belly), Kakergetes ("malefactor") because this king, who reigned in Egypt from 145 to 116 B.C., was reported by Greek writers to have been a monster of cruelty and licentiousness. Zabinas defeated Demetrius II Nicator, but was defeated in 122 B.C. and killed by Antiochus VIII, called Grypos ("hook nose"), who himself reigned at Antioch from 125 to 96 B.C. Hyrcanos, son of Simon Maccabaeus, reigned from 134 to 104 B.C.

IN THE YEAR 200 B.C. The Lacedaemonians (or Spartans) refused to take part in the expedition of Alexander the Great which resulted in the Hellenization of Asia. Plutarch, in his "Life of Alexander the Great," says that "generally upon all the . . . spoils [Alexander] put this honorable inscription: Alexander the son of Philip and the Grecians, excepting the Lacedaemonians, have won this spoile upon the barbarous Asians." In the poem, a Greek is supposed to be reading this inscription in 200 B.C. The three battles in which Alexander overthrew the Persians were fought at the River Granicus (334 B.C.), at Issus (333 B.C.), and near Arbela (331 B.C.) See Plutarch's "Life of Alexander the Great."

IN THE SUBURBS OF ANTIOCH. The Christians of Antioch had buried the body of their bishop, Babylas, illegally in the gardens of the Temple of Daphne near Antioch. Julian ordered the body to be removed. That very night, the temple was destroyed by fire. See Julian's *Misopôgôn* (*Julian*, Loeb Classics, Vol. 2, p. 484).

EARLY POEMS

WHEN, MY FRIENDS, I WAS IN LOVE. In rhyme, abab cdcd efef ghgh.

BACCHIC. In rhyme, aabb ccbb eebb ggbb hhbb.

THE POET AND THE MUSE. In rhyme, abab cdcd efef ghgh ijij klkl mnmn.

BUILDERS. In rhyme, abab cdcd eee fff.

SHAM-EL-NESSIM. In rhyme, aabcaabc defdfe ghigih ajjajj klmkml nopnpo qrsqsr aabcaabc. Sham-el-Nessim is an annual spring festival which goes back to the wheat harvest festival of ancient Egypt, and coincides with the Orthodox Easter Monday, when Egyptians and Christians go to the countryside and join together in merrymaking. Khabari is a slum section in Alexandria. Mahmoudiya is the name of a canal on the outskirts of Alexandria. The Mex is a beach in Alexandria. Muharram Bey is the name of a district in Alexandria, once aristocratic. Ptah is chief god of Memphis. The Ramleh is the main residential section of Alexandria.

SINGER. In rhyme, abab abab aaa bbb.

VULNERANT OMNES ULTIMA NECAT (All Wound, the Last One Slays). In rhyme, aabb cdeefccdfhiih jjkklmcmcl.

GOOD AND BAD WEATHER. In rhyme, abcdda abceea.

ELEGY OF THE FLOWERS. In rhyme, abbba accca addda aeeea afffa.

MELANCHOLY HOURS. In rhyme, abbac deedc fggfe.

TO THE MOON. In rhyme, abccbadd.

THE INKWELL. In rhyme, abba cddc effe ghhg, and so on.

ATHENA'S VOTE. The source of this poem is the trial of Orestes before the

Areopagus, dramatized by Aeschylus in *The Eumenides*. At this trial, the votes of the judges were equally divided, and Athena gave her deciding vote for acquittal. The trial signified the replacement of blood feud by state intervention and formal trial. Metis (prudence, wisdom, skill) was the first wife of Zeus.

BY THE OPEN WINDOW. In rhyme, abaacbccddeffgghehii.

ODE AND ELEGY OF THE ROADS. In rhyme, abcdd abcdd.

IN THE HOUSE OF THE SOUL. In rhyme, abcacab defdfde.

THERE IS A BLESSED JOY. In alternate rhymes.

OUR DEAREST WHITE YOUTH. In rhyme, aabbcddc eeffghhg.

ADDITION. In rhyme, aabcbc.

THE BANK OF THE FUTURE. In rhyme, aab bcc.

DEATH OF EMPEROR TACITUS. In rhyme, abbac deedc. Marcus Claudius Tacitus was Roman emperor from A.D. 275 to 276.

THE TEARS OF PHAETON'S SISTERS. In alternate rhyme. Phaeton, son of Apollo and the nymph Clymene, persuaded his father to let him drive the chariot of the sun across the heavens, but he lost control and, approaching too near the earth, set it on fire. To save the earth from complete destruction, Zeus killed him with a lightning bolt. He fell headlong into the Eridanus River. His weeping sisters, the Heliades, were turned into poplar trees and their tears into amber.

HORACE IN ATHENS. In rhyme, abbb accc abba ee.

THE TARANTINIANS CAROUSE. In rhyme, aaabbb acac.

VOICE FROM THE SEA. In rhyme, abab ccdeed ffghhg ccdhhd iijkkkj abab llmnnm oopqqp llrssr ttuvvvu.

INTERVENTION OF THE GODS. In rhymed couplets.

ARTIFICIAL FLOWERS. In rhyme, abaab cdcd efeef ghgh. In a letter to his friend Pericles Anastasiades, to whom he had sent a copy of this poem, Cavafy wrote, in English: "'Artificial Flowers' is a flight to the lovely realm of pure Fantasy and Extravaganza. One turn of expression in the 5th line is, I think, good—'their ephemeral flesh.' 'Flowers flesh' does not sound commonplace." The word "ephemeral" is not in the printed version of the poem.

BIBLIOGRAPHY

ENGLISH

C. M. Bowra, "Constantine P. Cavafy," *The Creative Experiment*, London, Macmillan, 1949

E. M. Forster, *Pharos and Pharillon*, London, Hogarth Press, 1923

E. M. Forster, "The Poetry of C. P. Cavafy," *Athene*, June 4, 1943

Francis Golffing, "The Alexandrian Mind," *Partisan Review*, Winter, 1955

Horace Gregory, "The Poetry of Cavafy," *Poetry*, March, 1953

Edmund Keeley and Philip Sherrard, *Six Poets of Modern Greece*, New York, Alfred A. Knopf, 1961

Robert Lidell, "Studies in Genius: Cavafy," *Horizon*, July–December, 1948

John Mavrogordato, *The Poems of C. P. Cavafy*, introduction by Rex Warner, London, Hogarth Press, 1951; New York, Grove Press, 1952

Kimon Friar, "One of the Greats," *New Republic*, January 26, 1953

Edouard Roditi, "The Poetry of C. P. Cavafy," *Poetry*, March, 1953

Philip Sherrard, "Constantine Cavafis," *The Marble Threshing Floor*, London, Vallentine, Mitchell, 1956

C. G. Tarelli, "Cavafis," *Link*, June, 1939

C. A. Trypanis, *Medieval and Modern Greek Poetry*, Oxford, Clarendon Press, 1951

FRENCH

Samuel Baud-Bauvy, *Poésie de la Grèce Moderne*, Lausanne, La Concorde, 1946

Theodore Griva, *Poèmes de C. P. Cavafis*, Lausanne, Abbáye du Livre, 1947

Georges Papoutsakis, *Poèmes de C. P. Cavafy*, Paris, Society d'Edition, Les Belles Lettres, 1958

Pierre Sephers, "Un Poète Grec Moderne, Constantine Cavafis," *Le Nef*, October–December, 1948

Marguerite Yourcenar and Constantin Dimaras, *Presentation Critique de Constantin Cavafy*, Paris, Gallimard, 1958

GREEK

K. P. Kabaphēs, *Poiēmata (Poems)*, Athens, Ikaros, 1952

K. P. Kabaphēs, *Poiēmata (Poems)*, Alexandria, Henōsis Hellenōn Logotehnōn (Society of Hellenic Men of Letters), 1935

Konstantinos P. Kabaphēs, "Prota Poiēmata" *(anekdota)* ("Early Poems," unpublished), Athens, *Ta Nea Grammata*, January and February, 1936

Ariston Kampani, *Istoria Tis Neas Hellenikis Logotehnias (History of Modern Greek Literature)*, 4th edition, Athens, Kallaros & Sons, 1903

Timos Malanos, *O Poietēs K. P. Kabaphēs (The Poet C. P. Cavafis)*, Athens, Gobosti Publications, Athens, 1933

Timos Malanos, *Peri Kabaphē (About Cavafy)*, Athens, Typographio Sergiade, 1935

Michael Peridis, *O Bios kai to Ergo tou Konstantinou Kabaphē (The Life and Work of Constantine Cavafy)*, Athens, Ikaros, 1948

Thrasyboulos Stavrou, *Neohellenike Metrike (Modern Greek Metrics)*, Athens, I. N. Sidere, 1930

Stratis Tsirkas, *O Kabaphēs kai H Epohí tou (Cavafy and His Epoch)*, Athens, Kedros, 1958

ITALIAN

Filippo Maria Pontani, "Metrica di Cavafes," *Reale Accademia de Scienze Lettere e Arti Di Palermo*, Serie IV, Vol. 5, Parte II, Palermo, 1944–45